DK EYEWITNESS TRAVEL

TOP 10
NAPLES
& THE AMALFI COAST

JEFFREY KENNEDY

DK | Penguin
Random
House

Top 10 Naples and the Amalfi Coast Highlights

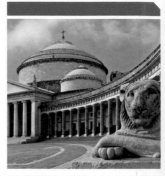

The Top 10 of Everything

CONTENTS

Naples and the Amalfi Coast Area by Area

Streetsmart

The information in this DK Eyewitness Top 10 Travel Guide is checked regularly. Every effort has been made to ensure that this book is as up-to-date as possible at the time of going to press. Some details, however, such as telephone numbers, opening hours, prices, gallery hanging arrangements and travel information are liable to change. The publishers cannot accept responsibility for any consequences arising from the use of this book, nor for any material on third party websites, and cannot guarantee that any website address in this book will be a suitable source of travel information. We value the views and suggestions of our readers very highly. Please write to: Publisher, DK Eyewitness Travel Guides, Dorling Kindersley, 80 Strand, London WC2R 0RL, Great Britain, or email travelguides@dk.com

Within each Top 10 list in this book, no hierarchy of quality or popularity is implied. All 10 are, in the editor's opinion, of roughly equal merit.

Front cover and spine *The Santa Maria Assunta church in Positano*
Back cover *Church San Francesco di Paola in Naples*
Title page *View of the coastline from Villa Rufolo, Ravello*

Welcome to
Naples and
the Amalfi Coast

From the vibrant streets of the city to sun-kissed beaches, dramatic cliff-hugging roads, ancient temples and island paradises, Naples and the Amalfi Coast is a hive of historical, cultural and natural beauty. With Eyewitness Top 10 Naples and the Amalfi Coast, the region is yours to explore.

It's hard not to fall in love with this region: the colours, the history, the beauty. What could be better than watching the sun setting across the Bay of Naples from the **Castel dell'Ovo**, uncovering historical treasures at the **Museo Archeologico Nazionale**, devouring a Neapolitan pizza hot from the oven, seeing the pastel-coloured cascade of homes in **Positano** or sipping a *limoncello* in **Amalfi**? It's all here, packed into an unforgettably beautiful landscape.

Be sure to take time during your stay to explore the cultural and artistic treasures that lie just moments from the coast. Step back in time at the ancient towns of **Pompeii** and **Herculaneum** or visit the best-preserved Greek temples in the world at **Paestum**. Escape to the island of **Capri** for spectacular natural beauty and to soak in the warm waters of the Mediterranean Sea, or get lost amidst the grandeur of the **Reggia di Caserta**. With so much to see and do, this is one of Italy's most diverse and seductive areas to discover.

Whether you're here for a weekend or a week, our Top 10 guide has all you'll need to experience everything the region has to offer, from the lively streets of **Spaccanapoli** to the panoramic vistas of **Ravello**. With travel tips throughout the guide, along with five itineraries, detailed maps and inspiring photography, this is the essential pocket-sized travel companion for your journey. **Enjoy the book, and enjoy Naples and the Amalfi Coast**.

Clockwise from top: **Procida Island; Spaccanapoli, Naples; Villa Cimbrone, Ravello; bird's-eye view of Amalfi; fresco inside Villa dei Misteri, Pompeii; Blue Grotto, Capri; Temple of Hera, Paestum**

Exploring Naples and the Amalfi Coast

One of Italy's most vibrantly diverse regions, Naples and the Amalfi Coast offer a wealth of artistic treasures, culture and natural beauty to discover. Here are some ideas to make the most of your stay, from an intensive weekend break in Naples to a wide-ranging week itinerary of the area.

Two Days in Naples

Day ❶
MORNING

Start in the heart of Royal Naples (see pp86–9) at the grandiose Piazza del Plebiscito. Visit the **Palazzo Reale** (see pp12–13), climb the ramparts of the **Castel Nuovo** (see pp14–15), imagine the sparkling lights at **Teatro San Carlo** (see p89) and stroll through the **Galleria Umberto I** (see p88). Stop for lunch at Brandi, known as the birthplace of Neapolitan pizza (see p93).

AFTERNOON

Revel in the vibrant atmosphere of **Spaccanapoli** (see pp76–9) and see the impressive **Duomo** (see pp16–17), majolica-tiled cloister of **Santa Chiara** (see p77) and "Veiled Christ" statue at the **Sansevero Chapel** (see p79).

Day ❷
MORNING

Step back in time at the fascinating Roman ruins of **Pompeii** (see pp30–31) or **Herculaneum** (see pp32–3). Then climb to the top of **Mount Vesuvius** (see p95) for an unforgettable view of the Bay of Naples.

Capodimonte Museum

0 metres 500
0 yards 500

From Herculaneum

Museo Archeologico Nazionale

Museo Metro Station

Duomo

Sansevero Chapel

Santa Chiara

SPACCANAPOLI

Castel Sant'Elmo, Certosa di San Martino

Galleria Umberto I

Municipio Metro

Teatro San Carlo

Castel Nuovo

Brandi

Piazza del Plebiscito

Palazzo Reale

Spaccanapoli cuts a pathway through the heart of Naples.

Castel dell'Ovo

Borgo Marinari

Key
— Two-day itinerary
— Seven-day itinerary

Clinging to the hillside, Positano is a stunning backdrop to the sandy beach.

AFTERNOON
Return to Naples to see the ancient treasures at the **Museo Archeologico Nazionale** *(see pp18–21)* – closed Tuesdays. Enjoy dinner in the romantic Borgo Marinari surrounded by fishing boats and the **Castel dell'Ovo** *(see p88)*.

Seven Days in Naples and the Amalfi Coast

Days ❶ and ❷
As Two Days in Naples.

Day ❸
Head to Naples' highest district to visit the **Certosa di San Martino** *(pp26–9)* and **Castel Sant'Elmo** *(see p89)*. Art lovers won't want to miss the **Capodimonte Museum** *(see pp22–3)* – closed Wednesdays.

Day ❹
If desired, transfer your base to the Amalfi Coast and explore **Amalfi** *(see pp36–7)*, with its impressive Cathedral of St Andrew and fascinating Museo della Carta. High in the mountains above Amalfi, visit the peaceful town of **Ravello** for its fine gardens and views *(see pp36–7)*.

Day ❺
Enjoy a drive along the Amalfi Coast road from **Sorrento** *(see p102)* to **Salerno** *(see p102)*, or take a ferry to soak up the sun in **Positano**, known as the "Vertical City" *(see pp36–7)*.

Day ❻
Take the ferry to **Capri** *(see pp34–5)* where highlights include the famous Blue Grotto, spectacular views from Monte Solaro in Anacapri, the picturesque Marina Piccola and shopping in Capri Town.

Day ❼
Discover the ancient Greek ruins of **Paestum** *(see pp38–9)* and visit the excellent museum on site here.

The Greco-Roman site of Paestum contains the fascinating remains of three ancient Greek temples.

Top 10 Naples and the Amalfi Coast Highlights

Ruins of the Roman forum, Pompeii, backed by Mount Vesuvius

TOP 10 Naples and the Amalfi Coast Highlights

This area is an anomaly – one of the earth's most beautiful and yet most accursed places. It has been the choice of the wealthy as their playground, while also being the scene of some of the greatest natural disasters. Naples itself is a vibrant urban setting, almost non-European in its intensity, while the beauty of the coast has been known to make men weep.

Palazzo Reale ①
With its commanding position near the bay, the Royal Palace dominates the grandest part of the city *(see pp12–13)*.

Castel Nuovo ②
Despite its bulky towers of volcanic stone, this Renaissance castle also features one of the most graceful archway entrances of the period, carved in the purest white marble *(see pp14–15)*.

Duomo ③
Naples' cathedral boasts a treasure-laden Palaeo-Christian basilica from the 4th century. The side chapel, dedicated to the city's adored patron saint San Gennaro, is huge and resplendent *(see pp16–17)*.

Museo Archeologico Nazionale ④
This is the repository of ancient art that has been unearthed from Pompeii and other digs in the area. The finds evoke a Classical civilization of refinement and grandeur *(see pp18–21)*.

Capodimonte ⑤
An unassuming hunting lodge that soon grew to become a vast royal palace. It now houses one of Italy's finest collections of art *(see pp22–3)*.

Certosa di San Martino

⑥ If there is one museum that captures the true Naples, this is it. Come for peerless views, for the masterpieces of the Neapolitan Baroque and the world's finest collection of nativity figures *(see pp26–9)*.

Pompeii and Herculaneum

⑦ The world-famous archaeological site comprises an entire culture caught in a moment when Vesuvius erupted nearly 2,000 years ago *(see pp30–33)*.

Capri

⑧ This small island has had a fabled history of glamour and decadence yet it still remains essentially a simple place *(see pp34–5)*.

Amalfi, Ravello and Positano ⑨

These three villages are a big draw along this rugged coastline known for its captivating natural beauty *(see pp36–7)*.

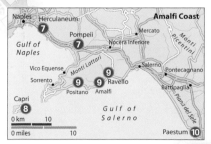

Paestum ⑩

Some of the best preserved Greek temples in the world stand in timeless splendour on this evocative plain south of Naples *(see pp38–9)*.

⭐ Palazzo Reale, Naples

One glance at this imposing royal palace and it becomes clear that, in its heyday, Naples was one of Europe's most important cities and home to one of the Mediterranean's most glittering royal courts. Begun in 1600, it was designed by Domenico Fontana and completed in two years. Additions, including the grand staircase, were made over the years, and it was redesigned in the 18th and 19th centuries. The edifice was a royal residence until 1946, when the monarchy was exiled for its ill-considered support of Mussolini's Fascist regime.

1 Façade
Dominating the vast Piazza del Plebiscito, the palace's late Renaissance façade **(above)** of brickwork and grey piperno stone is adorned with giant statues of Naples' foremost kings.

2 Decor of the Apartments
The theme of the frescoes that adorn the 30 royal apartments was chosen to flatter royals from various houses.

3 Biblioteca Nazionale
In the eastern wing, the massive National Library has at its core the Farnese collection, with books dating from the 5th century. Also here are 1st-century-BC papyri found at Herculaneum.

4 Staircase
The monumental staircase **(left)** leads from the central courtyard up to the royal apartments. The original masterpiece dates from 1651; in 1837 it was embellished with pink and white marble.

5 Furnishings
Fine examples of Empire furniture **(above)** predominate in the palace's apartments, much of it of French manufacture. Tapestries adorn many rooms, as do exceptional examples of 18th-century marble tables elaborately inlaid with semiprecious stones.

6 Sala di Ercole
The Hall of Hercules derives its name from the ancient statue displayed here in the 19th century.

Plan of Palazzo Reale

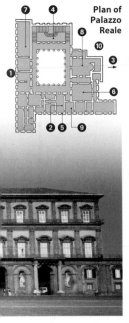

Cappella Palatina (8)

A 16th-century wooden door, painted in faux bronze, leads to the Royal Chapel **(right)**, where the court's religious activities took place. The high altar consists of semiprecious stones set in gilt copper, while the 18th-century nativity scene is a study of local life at the time.

Paintings (9)

Of considerable importance is the abundance of paintings of all genres, including works by Giordano, Guercino, Carracci, Preti and Titian. Also of interest are 17th-century Dutch portraits, 18th-century Chinese watercolours and 19th-century Neapolitan landscape paintings.

Gardens and Stables (10)

Located to the north of the palace, the gardens, which were laid out in 1841, afford great views of the hill of San Martino in one direction, and of Vesuvius and the bay in the other. The old stables here are now used for special exhibitions.

Teatrino di Corte (7)

Dating from 1768, this beautiful private theatre **(right)** attests to the royal family's passion for comic opera. In the side niches are 12 figures by Angelo Viva that depict Apollo and his Muses.

NEED TO KNOW

MAP N5 ■ Piazza del Plebiscito ■ 081 40 05 47 ■ DA

Open 9am–8pm Mon–Tue, Thu–Sun (last entry 7pm)

Adm €4

■ Caffè Gambrinus *(see p93)*, located in the stylish piazza next to the palace, is an excellent and historic choice for a drink, snack or a full meal.

■ The ticket office is notoriously hard to find, often confused with the gift shop. It's located on the side of the building, where the palace meets the San Carlo Opera House.

■ It's best to buy a Campania Artecard *(see p71)* – it reduces entrance fees to the major sights and you will also often get prioritized entry, saving a great deal of time.

Guide to the Palazzo Reale

You are free to walk around the inner courtyard and gardens at your leisure, without a ticket, as well as to enter the National Library. To visit the Royal Apartments, buy your ticket and take the grand staircase up to the left only, after which you may see the rooms in whatever order you wish and stay as long as you like.

🔟 ⭐ Castel Nuovo, Naples

The Castel Nuovo is more commonly known locally as the Maschio Angioino, a name that dates the fortress's origins to the reign of Charles I of Anjou in the late 13th century. It was officially called the "New Castle" to distinguish it from existing ones, namely the Ovo and the Capuano. During the reign of Robert of Anjou, the place became an important cultural centre, attracting such greats as Petrarch, Boccaccio and Giotto for productive sojourns. It was the Spanish conquerors from Aragon who, in the 15th century, gave it its present-day militaristic look as well as Renaissance embellishments.

Architecture ①
In the 15th century five cylindrical towers were added **(right)**, as was a Catalan courtyard and the Hall of the Barons.

② Triumphal Arch
Inspired by Roman antecedents, the arch **(above)** was built in 1443 to celebrate King Alfonso V of Aragon and features sculpted bas-reliefs.

③ Cappella Palatina
The castle's main chapel houses frescoes from the 14th to 16th centuries, as well as a fine Renaissance sculpted tabernacle.

④ Museo Civico
On the first floor here are paintings and sculptures **(below)**, including a 16th-century *Adoration of the Magi* in which the Wise Men are portraits of kings Ferrante I and Alfonso II, and Emperor Charles V. Also here are 15th-century bronze doors, depicting royal victories over rebellious barons.

⑤ Sala dei Baroni
In 1486 Ferrante I of Aragon invited barons who were plotting against him to a ball here, whereupon he had them all executed. Today the hall is notable for its splendid vaults **(above)**.

Plan of Castel Nuovo

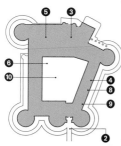

8 Paintings of Naples

The second floor of the museum focuses on Neapolitan works of a secular nature from the 18th to 20th centuries. Sculptures include *scugnizzi* (street urchins), especially the famous *Fisherboy* by Vincenzo Gemito.

9 Dungeons

Legend has it that prisoners would regularly disappear from these dungeons without a trace. The cause was discovered to be a huge crocodile that would grab their legs through a drain hole and drag them away; the hole now has a grating over it.

FROM FORTRESS TO CIVIC PARK

The castle still retains a defensive look – most notably the sloping base surmounted by a rim of castellated battlements. In the 16th century an enclosing ring wall was added, with bastions of its own, which hid the castle from view and gave the entire area an even more ominous feel. Following Italy's Unification, however, the outer wall was demolished and the area was laid out with avenues, lawns and flower gardens, lessening the forbidding aspect of the place.

6 Excavations

In the left corner of the courtyard visitors can view archaeological excavations through a glass floor. Macabre surprises include skeletons of monks from an early convent on the site.

7 Views

One of the best aspects of a visit to the castle is taking in the magnificent views from its upper walls and terraces. Panoramas include Mount Vesuvius and, on a clear day, even the Sorrentine Peninsula.

10 Inner Courtyard

This harmonious space **(above)** has typically Catalan features, such as the "depressed" arches – broader and flatter than Italian types – and an external grand staircase.

NEED TO KNOW

MAP N5 ■ Piazza Municipio ■ 081 795 58 77 ■ DA (partial)

Open 9am–8pm Mon–Sat (last entry 7pm)

Adm adults €4; between 18–24 year-olds €2

■ Inside nearby Galleria Umberto I is Caffè Roma, where you'll find a tempting array of drinks and freshly made local dishes *(see p88)*.

■ Sometimes sections of the castle can be closed, but enquire at the information office located in the courtyard and someone may be kind enough to let you in for a quick look.

🔟⭐ Duomo, Naples

Naples' cathedral originally dates from the 4th century AD with the founding of the Basilica of Santa Restituta, but two centuries later the Basilica del Salvatore was built at right angles to the first and this is the site now occupied by the Duomo. Work on the Duomo as it is seen today began in the 13th century during the reign of Charles I of Anjou, but over the centuries it has suffered repeated earthquake damage and has been restored according to prevailing tastes of the times. The result is a rich array of art and architecture going back 2,000 years. Next to the Duomo is the Museum of the Treasure of San Gennaro.

Interior and Ceiling ①

The interior cathedral never fails to dazzle. The floorplan is 100 m (330 ft) long, with a nave and two aisles lined with chapels **(right)**. Sixteen pillars support arches flanked by granite columns.

② Façade and Portals

The façade of Naples' cathedral **(above)** is a Neo-Gothic affair restored in the early 20th century but it is graced by three portals that date back to the 1400s.

③ Font

The cathedral's main baptismal font dates from 1618. The basin is made of Egyptian basalt, and there are Greek sculptures and an episcopal throne dating from 1376 in the right-hand nave.

④ Cappella di San Gennaro

Built in the 1600s, this Baroque extravaganza to the centre-right of the nave employed marble and precious metals and the great artists of the day to decorate its exquisite walls and domed ceiling **(right)**.

6 Cappella Minutolo

This chapel is one of the best-preserved examples of the Gothic style of the 13th and 14th centuries. The Cosmatesque mosaic floor **(left)** and altar frescoes are of particular note.

7 Relics

The main reliquary is a gold bust of San Gennaro containing his skull bones. There is also a vial containing small ampoules of his blood.

8 Santa Restituta

Naples' oldest building was commissioned by Emperor Constantine, who made Christianity the religion of the Roman Empire. Inside are a Romanesque fresco and mosaics dating from 1322.

9 Crypt of the Succorpo

The complexity and originality of this divine Renaissance chapel have led scholars to attribute the design to Bramante.

10 Baptistry

This is the oldest baptistry in the western world. It was built towards the end of the 4th century and is adorned with splendid mosaics **(above)**. The font is thought to have come from an ancient temple to Dionysus.

5 Archaeological Area

From Santa Restituta, you can enter the archaeological area, with remnants of Greek, Roman and early Christian structures, including walls, columns, mosaics, religious buildings and Greek and Roman roads. There is some evidence of *insulae* (apartment blocks) having been here in Roman times.

SAN GENNARO

Naples' patron saint was an early Christian who battled the disapproval of Emperor Diocletian. Bent on stamping out the off-shoot Jewish sect, Diocletian set about slaughtering Christians, but Gennaro survived by his faith until he was beheaded in AD 305. His body and vials of blood were preserved in the Catacombs of San Gennaro *(see p63)* until they were moved here. Later, a believer found that his dried blood miraculously liquefied on demand, an event that became a city-wide cult.

NEED TO KNOW

MAP P1 ▪ Via Duomo 147 ▪ 081 44 90 97

Duomo: 8:30am–1:30pm, 2:30–7:30pm Mon–Sat, 8:30am–1:30pm, 4:30–7:30pm Sun

Archaeological Area and Baptistry: 10:30am–5pm Mon, Tue, Thu–Sat, 9am–3pm Sun. Adm €3

Museum of the Treasure of San Gennaro: 9am–5pm Mon, Tue, Thu–Sun (Wed open for groups by appointment). Adm €7, under 18s and over 65s free

▪ For pizza without queues, visit Pizzeria Lombardi *(see p85)*.

▪ You will encounter large groups being led around by docents. No one will mind if you join the group; otherwise, take your own personal tour to another part of the cathedral until the crowds move on.

🔟⭐ Museo Archeologico Nazionale, Naples

Among the world's top museums of ancient art, Naples' Archaeological Museum overwhelms with its wealth of beautiful and priceless objects. The building was built in the 16th century as headquarters for the royal cavalry and later turned into a museum to house the Farnese Collection and the finds that were brought to light at Pompeii and Herculaneum. Now the Farnese Collection is broken up, with the paintings at Capodimonte and the books in the National Library, leaving this museum to focus on its ancient marvels.

Mosaics ④
Romans loved mosaics **(right)** on both floors and walls. Small chips of coloured glass and stone *(tesserae)* were used to create scenes of every genre.

⑤ Glass and Stone Vessels
Masters at producing coloured and transparent glassware, the Romans carried these techniques to artistic heights. Highlights of the collection include the celebrated Farnese Cup, engraved in semiprecious stone with layers of agate and sard-onyx, and the blue vase. Used as a wine vessel, the vase was found in a Pompeii tomb.

① Pottery and Metal Vessels
Pottery here includes Greek and Etruscan *kraters*, Roman terracotta jars, vases and figurines. Grecian urns, with red figures on black backgrounds, depict a variety of scenes **(above)**.

② Marble Sculpture
Replicas of some of the most renowned ancient Classical sculptures are housed here by artists such as Phidias, Lysippus, Praxiteles and Polyclitus. Also of great importance are the striking Greek and Roman busts.

③ Il Gabinetto Segreto
This collection showcases erotic art from Pompeii and Herculaneum. The exuberant sexuality of the ancient world inspired the frescoes, sculptures and mosaics on display.

⑥ Friezes, Frescoes and Murals
These Roman works **(above)** were excavated from Pompeii and disclose a great deal about the society and religion of the time.

7 Weapons, Jewellery, and Domestic Items

Shields, helmets **(right)** and swords remind us that the ancient world was one of combat, but metalsmiths also made adornments such as armlets. Domestic items include lamps and cups.

8 Egyptian and Prehistoric Items

This collection contains art from the Ancient Kingdom (2700–2200 BC) to the Roman age. Funereal sarcophagi and mummies can be seen here.

BUILDING THE COLLECTION

The Farnese Collection, inherited by King Ferdinando IV from his mother in the 18th century, forms the core of the museum, including one of the most important and largest groups of Roman antiquities in existence. Excavations around Vesuvius *(see pp30–31)* added to the bounty. In the past 200 years the inventory of world-class treasures has been augmented by many important aristocratic collections, including the Bourbon, Borgia, Orsini, Picchianti and Astarita collections.

9 Incised Gems, Coins and Epigraphs

The collection of incised gems contains Greek and Roman pieces; bronze, silver and gold coins **(below)**, including some from Magna Graecia. Ancient written records include the *Tavole di Eraclea* (3rd century BC).

10 Bronze Sculpture

This collection is a true treasure-trove of bronze masterpieces. The works include a Resting Hermes, Fauns, Water-Bearers and a host of statues and busts.

NEED TO KNOW

MAP N1 ■ Piazza Museo 19 ■ 081 442 21 49 ■ cir.campania. benicultural.it ■ DA (partial)

Open 9am–7:30pm Wed–Mon (ticket office closes 6:30pm)

Adm €10

Il Gabinetto Segreto: open for tours 9:30am–7:30pm Wed–Mon

■ Head for Piazza Bellini and sit outside Caffè Arabo *(see p83)* to gaze at the excavated Greek walls in the centre of the piazza.

■ Make an appointment to tour Il Gabinetto Segreto at the entrance to the museum. You will be given a time and a choice of languages.

■ At certain times, sections may close due to ongoing excavations.

TOP 10 Individual Masterpieces

1 Farnese Hercules
Created and signed by Glykon of Athens, this powerful marble sculpture is a copy and enlargement of a lost bronze original by the 4th-century BC Greek master Lysippus. It was also found in the ruins of the Baths of Caracalla in Rome, where it is thought that it served as magnificent decoration for the imperial pleasure-dome. The work shows the mythical hero at rest, exhausted after having completed his round of 12 super-human tasks. Ground floor.

2 Farnese Bull
Found in the Baths of Caracalla in Rome during excavations, this is the largest sculptural group to have survived from antiquity to date. One of the best-known pieces in the Farnese Collection, it recounts the story of Dirce (the first wife of Lykos, King of Thebes, who ill-treated Antiope and is being punished by the latter's sons by being tied to a bull. It is probably a copy – though some claim it may be the original – of a 2nd-century BC Greek work and is Hellenistic in its execution. Ground floor.

Alexander the Great mosaic

3 Alexander the Great Mosaic
Found as a floor decoration in Pompeii's Casa del Fauno, a grand aristocratic mansion of the 2nd century BC, this Hellenistic mosaic is certainly one of the most elegant and exciting to have survived. The subject is the routing of Darius's Persian armies by Alexander the Great's cavalry. The monumentality of the work is impressive and it is almost certainly a copy of a lost painting of great importance, possibly by Philoxeno. Fragmentary as it is, there are still some one million *tesserae* (tiles) in its composition. Mezzanine.

4 Dancing Faun
A more joyous image of freedom and exuberant health would be hard to imagine. This bronze was found in Pompeii's Casa del Fauno, to which it gives its name, as a decoration in the atrium to greet arriving guests. Two ancient replicas are known of this Hellenistic figure, so it must have been a popular and inspiring object. Mezzanine.

5 Hermes at Rest
Were it not for the wings on his feet, one might suppose that this very boyish Hermes (Mercury) was just a young athlete taking a break from his exertions rather than a god. The proportions of this sculpture were inspired by the work of Lysippus. First floor.

Farnese Bull sculpture

6 Sleeping and Drunken Satyrs

Satyrs to the ancients were always a symbol of pure hedonism – not just sexual licence, but every form of ease and indulgence. These two figures, from the Villa dei Papiri *(see p32)*, express a light-hearted indolence that is as implicitly erotic as it is earthy. The ancients believed that physical pleasure and delight were part of man's divine essence and gifts from the gods. First floor.

7 The Doryphoros

This is the most complete replica of the celebrated bronze original, created in about 440 BC by Polyclitus of Argos. The name means "spear-bearer" and one can see that the figure once held a spear in his left hand. It is thought to represent Achilles, and the statue was known in ancient times as the Canon, exhibiting perfect proportions in every aspect of its depiction of the human form. The sculptor developed a complex theory of measurements, related to music, for the ideal construction of the human body. Ground floor (sometimes on loan to other museums).

Prized exhibit, Farnese Cup

8 Farnese Cup

The star of the museum's cameo and incised gem collection is this glistening masterpiece, carved from a single piece of stone, specifically chosen by the artist for its layering of agate and sardonyx.

The outer face of the cup has an image of Medusa; inside is an allegorical scene that probably alludes to the fertility of the Nile. The cup was produced in Egypt in the 2nd or 1st century BC. Ground floor.

Famous fresco, Sacrifice of Iphigenia

9 Sacrifice of Iphigenia

Found in Pompeii, in the so-called House of the Tragic Poet, this famous painting shows the dramatic moment when the sacrifice of Iphigenia is halted by the intervention of Artemis (Diana), who kills a deer instead. The fresco was once considered a faithful copy of a painting by the Greek artist Timante, but it is now thought to be an original Roman depiction – due primarily to its overall lack of compositional unity. First floor (can sometimes be out on loan to other museums).

10 Achilles and Chiron

Retrieved from the so-called Basilica in Herculaneum, this fresco depicts the young hero of the Trojan War with his mentor, the centaur Chiron. Since this large work was decoration for a public building, the message is clear – heed the elemental forces of Nature (symbolized by the centaur) to find balance and fulfilment in life. The image is based on a famous sculptural group, probably Greek, now lost but known to have stood in ancient Rome, as recorded by Pliny the Elder. First floor.

TOP 10 ⭐ Capodimonte, Naples

Construction began on this royal palace, museum and porcelain factory in 1738, under architect Antonio Medrano, and it has been home to a large part of the Farnese Collection since 1759. After the French occupation in 1799 the collection was briefly dispersed, with some pieces taken to France, but they were later returned following the restoration of the Bourbons in 1815. With the Unification of Italy, in 1860, the palace and its treasures became the property of the House of Savoy and the residence of the Dukes of Aosta until 1947. It was opened to the public in 1957 and restored in 1996, with the Neapolitan and contemporary art galleries added in 1997.

1 Pre-14th- and 14th-Century Art

Most of the earliest Italian art in the museum was acquired in the 19th and 20th centuries. Important works include Simone Martini's lavish Gothic masterpiece *San Ludovico di Tolosa*.

The palace's ballroom, with its impressive chandelier

2 15th-Century Art

Powerful works here include Botticelli's *Madonna with Child and Angels* **(above)** and Bellini's sublime *Transfiguration*.

4 17th-Century Art

Strongest of all the works here is Caravaggio's *Flagellation of Christ* and Artemisia Gentileschi's horrifying *Judith and Holofernes* **(right)**.

3 16th-Century Art

Here you'll find a serene *Assumption of the Virgin* by Pinturicchio, an *Assumption* by Fra' Bartolomeo and works by Titian and Raphael.

5 18th-Century Art

Neapolitan artist Francesco Solimena is well represented here, especially by his opulent portrait of a courtier, Principe Tarsia Spinelli. Other canvases provide us with period views of Naples, its bay and other scenes, including one of Vesuvius in eruption by Pierre-Jacques-Antoine Volaire **(above)**.

6 Porcelain Parlour

Designed for Queen Maria Amalia. Painted and gilded porcelain assumes the shapes of festoons, musical instruments and figurative scenes.

7 Drawings and Graphic Works

Sketches and studies by great artists are here, including works by Fra' Bartolomeo, Raphael and Michelangelo. Open mornings only.

8 19th-Century and Modern Art

History paintings and landscapes dominate his part of the collection. Endearing are the sculptures of street urchins by Vincenzo Gemito, but the signature modern work is Andy Warhol's cheerfully garish *Vesuvius*.

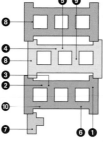

Key to Floorplan
- Mezzanine
- First floor
- Second floor
- Third floor

9 Decorative Arts

The palace is replete with decorative arts, from ivory carvings to tapestries, to 18th- and 19th-century furniture.

10 Palazzo Reale

First conceived as a hunting lodge by Charles Barbone, the palace **(above)** grew into a three-storey structure.

ROYAL PORCELAIN FACTORY

Charles of Bourbon established the Reale Fabbrica delle Porcellane in 1739 and it quickly became celebrated for the refinement of its porcelain creations. The factory flourished until 1759, when the king returned to his native Spain and took it and the staff with him, but it reopened in 1771, and production of top-quality pieces recommenced. The mark for objects made here was generally a crowned "N" in blue on the underside.

NEED TO KNOW

MAP K1 ■ Porta Grande via Capodimonte, Porta Piccola via Miano 2 ■ 081 749 91 11 ■ DA

Museum: 8:30am–7:30pm Thu–Tue (ticket desk closes 6:30pm). Adm €7.50 (€6.50 after 2pm)

Park: 8am–sunset daily

■ Choose the Museum Café for refreshment – it's located down the arcaded corridor away from the shop in the direction of the toilets and then right; follow the signs from there.

■ Public transport in Naples is not for the sensitive, and for most, the easiest way to get to the museum is by taxi. However, you can get there by bus: 178 runs from Via Toledo, R4 from Via Medina and C40 from Piazza Garibaldi.

Following pages Atrani, clinging to the cliffside

🔟 ⭐ Certosa di San Martino

In 1325 Charles, Duke of Calabria began construction on what is now one of the richest monuments in Naples, the monastery of San Martino. The extensive layout of the place, serenely ensconced just below the massive Castel Sant' Elmo, is nothing less than palatial, with two fine cloisters and a dazzling array of architectural and artistic wonders. The Carthusian monks were avid collectors and between the 16th and 18th centuries commissioned the greatest artists of the day to embellish their impressive edifice.

1 Façade
Although originally Gothic in style, the façade **(above)** has mostly been overlain with refined Baroque decoration, including the large round windows.

2 Choir and Sacristy
The richly carved walnut choir stalls were executed between 1629 and 1631 by Orazio de Orio and Giovanni Mazzuoli. Take note of the cherubs and the abundance of volute curves.

3 Church
The elaborate nave of the church **(below)** is a supreme display of Baroque art – the most complete record of Neapolitan art from the 17th and 18th centuries crowded into a single space.

5 Sculpture and Marble Decor

The altar, designed by Solimena, sports silver putti by Giacomo Colombo and silver angels by Sanmartino, who did many of the marble figures **(left)** that adorn the chapels.

THE MONASTERY'S GUARDIAN

Before entering the Certosa, be sure to take in the castle hovering above it. The monastery was built directly beneath Castel Sant'Elmo for the protection that it afforded. The original structure dates from Angevin times, but it was rebuilt by the Spanish in the 16th century on a six-pointed star design. Its original name was Sant'Erasmo, after the hill it stands on, but the name became corrupted over the centuries, first to Sant'Eramo, then Sant'Ermo, and finally to Sant'Elmo.

Beautiful view from the monastery's gardens

4 Gardens and Belvederes

One of the best aspects of the Certosa are its gardens. Not only are the views from here picture-perfect, but the gardens themselves are lush and fragrant.

Plan of the Monastery

6 Chapels and Subsidiary Rooms

The eight chapels are decorated in a unified style consistent with the main part of the church. All of them are rich with brightly coloured marble and opulent gilded stucco trim.

7 Quarto del Priore

These were the quarters of the monastery's Prior, spiritual leader and the only one of the monks who was allowed contact with the outside world. Aristocratic furnishings and priceless works of art from the Certosa collection adorn the walls.

8 Paintings and Frescoes

Dominating the ceiling is the *Ascension of Jesus* by Lanfranco, while the counter-façade has a lovely *Pietà* by Stanzione.

9 Chiostro Grande

The Large Cloister **(below)** is one of Italy's finest, with a 64-marble-columned portico that was designed in the 16th century.

10 Monks' Cemetery

In a corner of the Chiostro Grande is a plot where a small number of monks have been laid to rest.

Pinacoteca and Museum Exhibits

Triptych by Jean Bourdichon

1 Early International Renaissance Art

The most outstanding piece here is a triptych by Jean Bourdichon of the Virgin and Child and saints John the Baptist and John the Evangelist (c.1414). The work employs masterful perspective and anatomical detail.

2 Early Italian Renaissance Art

Of special note here is a 15th-century view of Naples, the *Tavola Strozzi*, by an unknown artist and the first painted view of the city from the sea. Sculptures include a marble *Madonna and Child*, attributed to Tino di Camaino.

3 High Renaissance Art

The most significant works here are marble sculptures, including a late 16th-century

Bernini's *Madonna with Child*

work by Pietro Bernini, *Madonna with Child and St John the Baptist as a Child*. Its twisting composition, with St John kissing the Child's foot and Mary looking on, embodies tenderness.

4 Baroque Art

This era is the collection's strongest suit. Significant sculptures include a *Veiled Christ* in terracotta by Corradini and a *St Francis* in marble by Sanmartino. A devout Lanfranco painting, *Madonna with Child and Saints Domenico and Gennaro*, is typical of the age.

5 Jusepe Ribera

The great Spanish artist, who worked in Naples for most of his life, was appreciated for his dramatic style *(see p45)*. His *St Sebastian* is one of the most powerful works, showing the ecstatic face of the young man, his body pierced with arrows.

6 Micco Spadaro

This artist's *Martyrdom of St Sebastian* provides an interesting contrast with Ribera's work. Rather than focus on the man in close-up, he is shown off to the right being tied up, just before Roman soldiers let their arrows fly. Another Spadaro work shows the monks of the

Tavola Strozzi, a 15th-century view of Naples from the sea

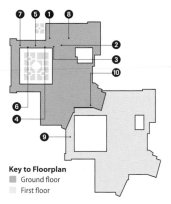

Key to Floorplan
- Ground floor
- First floor

The custom of nativity scenes is traditionally traced to December 1223, when St Francis of Assisi celebrated mass before a sculptured group of the Holy Family flanked by a live ox and ass. However, in 1025, there was already a church of Sancta Maria ad Praesepem in Naples, where a representation of the Nativity became the focus of devotion.

Called *presepio*, derived from the Latin *praesepe* or "feeding trough", referring to the Christ Child's initial resting place, the art of the nativity scene grew to become a major undertaking in the 1600s. Kings and queens would vie with each other to gather together the most impressive, dazzling, poignant and often humorous display, commissioning the best artists and designers of the day. It was not until the end of the 19th century that these wonderful works were fully recognized as an artistic genre in their own right.

The oldest example of a monumental Neapolitan *presepio* comes from the church of San Giovanni a Carbonara; sculpted by Pietro and Giovanni Alemanno in 1478–84, it originally included 41 life-size wooden figures, of which 19 still survive in the church.

Certosa thanking Christ for sparing them from the plague, with a view of Naples' bay through the arcades.

7 Stanzione

Stanzione's *Baptism of Christ* is noteworthy for the luminous way the flesh is rendered, employing pronounced effects of *chiaroscuro* (light and shade).

Nativity scene, Cuciniello Presepe

8 Nativity Collection

Of all the priceless nativity scenes and figures here, the Cuciniello Presepe is by far the most elaborate. Quite lost is the manger scene amid 180 shepherds, 10 horses, 8 dogs, folk going about their business, a Moroccan musical ensemble and much more. Lighting effects create dawn, day, dusk and night.

9 Glass, Porcelain and Gold

The array of objects here goes back to the 1500s and includes painted plates, vases, tiles, pitchers, mirrors and figurines. Subject matter ranges from religious, such as a coral and gold Crucifix, to mythological, to scenes from daily life.

10 Neapolitan 19th-Century Art

Pre- and post-Unification was a time when Italians awoke to their cultural heritage and began to capture it in art. City views and its environs are informative of bygone days, as are the portraits.

TOP10 ⭐ Pompeii

Two thousand years ago, few people knew that Vesuvius was a volcano, although in AD 62, what turned out to be a premonitory tremor caused damage to the coastal town of Pompeii as well as to other towns in the vicinity. Years later, residents were still repairing the damage to their homes and public buildings. Then, in AD 79, came the most devastating eruption *(see p33)*. Horrific as it was for those who suffered, the result was the preservation of an ancient culture like a time capsule to be discovered centuries later.

1 Forum
Every Roman city centred commercial, civic, political and religious life around the Forum **(right)**, generally a long rectangular area.

2 Amphitheatre
Far to the east stands Pompeii's amphitheatre – a typical oval shape, though small by Roman standards **(above)**. It was the first of its kind built for gladiatorial combat.

3 House of Menander
This grand house **(right)** includes an atrium, peristyle and baths. It proved to be a treasure-trove of silver objects, now on display in Naples' Museo Archeologico.

4 Theatre
The large 2nd-century BC theatre was built in the style of the Greek system, using the slope of the land for the *cavea* (seating area).

5 Stabian Baths
To the west of Via Stabiana are the Stabian Baths, the most ancient structure here, dating back to the 4th century BC. The stuccoed vaults in the men's changing room have preserved images of nymphs and cupids.

6 Brothel
The *lupanarium*, which is the largest of the ruined Roman city's brothels, is decorated with frescoes depicting erotic, sometimes explicit, acts, which help to give some clue to the proclivities of the prostitutes.

Map of Pompeii

7 House of the Vettii
One of the most beautiful houses in Pompeii, the interior is adorned with splendid paintings and friezes featuring mythological themes.

8 House of the Golden Cupids
This sumptuous house was named after the gold-leaf decorations of *amorini* (cupids) in the bedroom. It was owned by the Poppaea family, that of Nero's second wife. The gardens were adorned with sculptures, marble tables and a pool.

10 House of the Faun
The 1-m (3-ft) bronze statue of the Dancing Faun **(left)**, found here in the middle of the courtyard pond, accounts for the name of this house, which covered an entire *insula* (city block). Still here are *opus sectile* mosaic marble floors (coloured geometric patterns) as well as wall decorations of great merit.

9 Via dei Sepulcri and Villa dei Misteri
The Way of the Tombs lies outside the city gates for fear of the dead bringing bad luck. Beyond this is the 90-room House of the Mysteries, where you can peek in to see the marvellous wall paintings.

MOUNT VESUVIUS

In ancient times, Vesuvius was simply "the mountain", covered with vegetation and vines, until it famously blew its stack in AD 79. At least five other occurrences have been recorded in the last 400 years and experts estimate that it could erupt again at any time. Its last rumble was in 1944, when the pointed cone disappeared, along with the smoky plume that issued from it.

NEED TO KNOW

MAP E4 ■ 081 857 53 47 ■ Via Villa dei Misteri 2 ■ www.pompeiisites. org ■ DA (partial)

Open 9am–7:30pm daily (until 5pm Nov–Mar) (last entry 90 mins before closing time)

Herculaneum, Oplontis and Stabiae: 8:30am–7:30pm daily

Adm Pompeii €13, Herculaneum €11, Oplontis and Stabiae €5.50, cumulative ticket available €22

Villa dei Papiri: 9am–noon Sat–Sun; must book ahead at www.arethusa.net

Crater of Vesuvius: 9am–5pm daily. Guided tours (see p95). Adm €6.50

■ There are on-site cafés at Pompeii and Herculaneum.

■ Guided tours are also available – call 081 857 53 47.

■ Some houses may be subject to closure due to restoration work.

Herculaneum, Oplontis and Stabiae

1 Villa dei Papiri

The remains of the resort town of Herculaneum were discovered before Pompeii but were harder to excavate since it was covered by a thicker layer of volcanic ash. Fortunately, this also meant that every aspect was better preserved. This villa was one of the first to be explored, housing art treasures now in the Museo Archeologico (see pp18–21). The papyrus scrolls that give the villa its name are in the National Library.

Map of Herculaneum

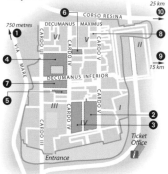

Art uncovered at Villa dei Papiri

2 House of the Stags

The name derives from the sculpture of stags being attacked by dogs that was found here. Other sculptures include a Satyr with Wineskin and a Drunken Hercules.

3 House of the Mosaic Atrium

This house takes its name from its mosaic floor of black-and-white geometric patterns. Gardens and rooms with views of the sea must have made it a lovely place to relax.

4 City Baths

Built in 10 BC, these traditional baths are fascinating. They are divided into male and female sections, both decorated with the same sea-themed mosaics featuring tritons and fish. At the centre of the complex is an open porticoed area used as a gymnasium.

5 Trellis House

This building provides a wonderfully preserved example of what an ordinary multi-family dwelling was like. Two storeys high, it has a balcony that overhangs the pavement and its walls are composed of wood and reed laths with crude tufa and lime masonry to fill in the frame.

6 House of Neptune and Amphitrite

This is named after the mosaic of the sea god and his nymph-bride that adorns the fountain in the summer dining room at the back of the house.

Mosaic decoration, City Baths

The eponymous mosaic, House of Neptune and Amphitrite

Other fine mosaics can be seen here too. The shop attached to the house has wooden structures and furniture in perfect condition.

7 House of the Wooden Partition

A kind of "accordion" partition here was devised to separate the atrium from the *tablinium*, the room of business affairs.

Marble counter tops, Thermopolia

8 Thermopolia

The Thermopolia is an example of a fast-food outlet of the day. The terracotta amphorae set into the marble counter top would have contained various comestibles. Only wealthy people had facilities to cook food, so most would stop by such a place to eat.

9 Villa of Sabina Poppaea and Villa of Crassus

These beautifully preserved aristocratic villas are located in what was once the ancient resort of Oplontis. The complex includes gardens, porticoes, private baths, a pool and astounding wall decorations.

THE ERUPTION OF AD 79

On 24 August AD 79, Mount Vesuvius suddenly erupted. The apex of the calamity started at about 10am and by 1pm it was all over – all the cities on the mountain's slopes were covered with lava, and Pompeii and its citizens were entirely buried. It lay undiscovered until 1750.

Here are the words of Pliny the Younger, who survived to write an eyewitness account of the events: "On Mount Vesuvius broad sheets of fire and leaping flames blazed at several points, their bright glare emphasized by the darkness… an ominous thick smoke, spreading over the earth like a flood, enveloping the earth in night… earth-shocks so violent it seemed the world was being turned upside down… the shrill cries of women, the wailing of children, the shouting of men… Many lifted up their hands to the gods, but a great number believed there were no gods, and that this was to be the world's last, eternal night…The flames and smell of sulphur… heralded the approaching fire …The dense fumes… choked… nearly everyone, to death."

10 Stabian Villas

Set on the Varano Hill just outside Castellammare di Stabia, both villas preserve mosaic floors, gardens, peristyles and frescoes. Villa Arianna is named after a fresco of Ariadne being abandoned by Theseus. Villa San Marco sports a gymnasium, pool and interesting frescoes.

⭐ Capri

Ever since ancient times, this luxuriant, saddle-shaped rock in the Bay of Naples has captured the world's imagination as a place where dreams can be realized and life can become an earthly paradise. Hopes and wishes notwithstanding, the island does have something special, perhaps generated by its sheer dramatic beauty, its crystal-clear waters and its lush vineyards and lemon and olive groves that seem to cover every available corner.

Marina Grande ①
Whether by ferry, hydrofoil or private yacht, virtually all visitors to the island arrive at this little port town – a mesmerizing sight as you approach **(right)**. It's a colourful place, but the bustle is only skin-deep – in reality it's just as laid back as the rest of Capri.

Capri Town ②
Piazza Umberto I, which is known simply as "Piazzetta" **(above)** is the town's outdoor salon, filled to the brim with chic bars and restaurants. Nighttime is when the true Capri denizens come out to play.

Villa Jovis ③
Emperor Tiberius's 1st-century-AD villa, built on the cliff's edge, is now in ruins **(right)** but the views of the Bay of Naples, from the highest point at this end of the island, are dazzling.

Arco Naturale ④
Follow signs from Capri Town for this easygoing walking trail, where rocky staircases offer fine panoramas of the mainland coastline. The Natural Arch itself consists of a huge limestone crag, jutting out and with the bright turquoise sea seen below.

Via Krupp and I Faraglioni ⑤
Via Krupp **(above)** is a switchback path carved into the cliff face. From here there are views of I Faraglioni rocks.

Marina Piccola ⑥
This small harbour has private bathing huts, a pebbly arc of beach, wonderful rocks for diving from and several good fish restaurants.

7 Monte Solaro

No trip to the island is complete without a chairlift ride up to Capri's highest peak, from which you can look down on the pastoral timelessness of lemon groves, little white houses, and endless flower gardens that cover the island – breathtaking.

8 Anacapri and Punta Carena

Before 1877, when the road was built, Anacapri was isolated and is still less pretentious than the rest of the island. From here, another great jaunt is to the lighthouse at Punta Carena, where a rocky beach awaits, as well as good facilities and restaurants.

9 Villa San Michele

Built by a Swedish doctor on the site of one of Tiberius's houses, Villa San Michele is an eclectic mix of Romanesque, Renaissance and Moorish styles, surrounded by gorgeous gardens.

A GLAMOROUS PAST

Capri emerged on the upmarket tourist map in the 19th century, but the high point of famed "Gay Capri" was the early 20th century, which is when it began to attract literati such as Norman Douglas, Graham Greene, Somerset Maugham and Maxim Gorky. Later on, the 1960s, the era known as "Capri People", brought the international jet-set to the island, including *La Dolce Vita* swingers, Hollywood film stars, and even the beautiful newly-wed Jacqueline Kennedy.

Map of Capri

Isola di Capri

ANACAPRI

CAPRI

10 Blue Grotto

The island's most famous attraction is this sea-grotto, of a colour and intensity of blue that can be experienced no-where else **(left)**. Local oarsmen ferry visitors inside – be aware that the grotto can close at short notice due to tide levels.

NEED TO KNOW

MAP C5 ■ Tourist Information: Piazzetta Cerno 11, 081 837 06 86, www.capritourism.com

Ferries and hydrofoils leave from many ports, including Mergellina and Beverello in Naples, Sorrento, Positano, Amalfi, Salerno, Ischia and Castellammare di Stabia.

Journey times to Capri: 80 mins from Naples; 40 mins from Sorrento. Hydrofoils take half these times.

■ In Capri town there are many good eating and drinking options in and around Piazzetta.

■ To get a feel for the island, take one of the recommended hikes – or better still, rent a kayak and go exploring along the otherwise inaccessible coastline areas.

■ Note that Villa Krupp can often be closed for safety reasons.

TOP 10 ⭐ Amalfi, Ravello and Positano

With its dramatic coastline dotted with villages clinging to cliffs that drop down to the azure sea, the beauty of the Amalfi Coast has been luring travellers since ancient times. Beyond the striking landscape lies a fascinating history in Amalfi, home to the powerful Republic of Amalfi in the Middle Ages. Positano's idyllic setting and pastel-hued homes draped with fauna leave an indelible mark, while Ravello is set boldly upon a rocky spur, suspended high above the sea.

1 Duomo di Amalfi

Sitting atop a staircase, Amalfi's cathedral **(below)** is dedicated to St Andrew and features the 13th-century Cloister of Paradise, museum, crypt and sumptuous Baroque interior.

2 Museo della Carta, Amalfi

Discover Amalfi's important role in the history of papermaking at this interesting small museum, which is evocatively set in a historic paper mill (see p49).

3 Valle delle Ferriere, Amalfi

Hike from Amalfi into the Valle delle Ferriere (Valley of the Mills) where ruins of once prosperous paper mills are surrounded by a lush forest.

NEED TO KNOW

MAP E5 ■ Tourist Information: Amalfi, Via delle Repubbliche Marinare, 089 87 11 07; Ravello, Via Roma 18, 089 85 70 96/79 77; Positano, Via Regina Giovanna 13, 089 87 50 67

Villa Cimbrone: Via Santa Chiara 26. 089 85 74 59. 9am–sunset daily. Adm €7

Villa Rufolo: Piazza del Duomo. 089 85 76 21. 9am–30 min before sunset daily. Adm €5

Duomo di Ravello: Piazza del Duomo. 089 85 83 11. Church 9am–1pm, 4–7pm daily; museum: 9am–7pm (summer), 9am–6pm (winter) daily. Adm €2

Duomo di Amalfi: Piazza Duomo. 089 87 13 24.

9am–7pm (summer), 10am–4pm (winter) daily. Adm €3

Museo della Carta: Via delle Cartiere 23. 089 830 45 61. 10am–6:30pm daily (summer), 10am–3:30pm daily except Mon and Thu (winter). Adm €4

Santa Maria Assunta: Via Marina Grande. 089 87 54 80. 8am–12pm, 4pm–8pm daily

4 Atrani

Amalfi's next-door neighbour to the east is the picturesque fishing village of Atrani **(below)**, which is one of Italy's smallest municipalities. The narrow alleys and main square are a flashback in time and the beach is an attractive alternative to Amalfi.

5 Scala

This tiny hamlet, built on a succession of terraces, is well worth a visit for the outstanding views it affords when you look back at its larger neighbour, Ravello.

Map of Amalfi and Ravello

6 Villa Cimbrone, Ravello

The creation of an English lord, Ernest Beckett, the house imitates the Moorish style that predominates in Ravello, and its gardens are set with Classical temples **(above)**.

7 Villa Rufolo, Ravello

The 800-year-old Arab-style palace and its lovely terraced gardens **(above)** have inspired lots of visitors. The terrace is used in summer for staging concerts.

8 Duomo di Ravello

The 11th-century cathedral is a treasure-trove of works. Its beautiful pulpit (1272) has twisted columns resting on sculpted lions at the base.

9 Santa Maria Assunta Church, Positano

With its multi-coloured majolica-tiled dome and shimmering white and gold Baroque interior, Positano's main church is as pretty as its setting.

10 Fornillo Beach, Positano

Follow the scenic pathway hugging the cliff to this beautiful beach set in a cove flanked by two watchtowers; the perfect respite from the summer crowds.

RAVELLO MUSIC FESTIVAL

Each summer Ravello is transformed into a haven for music lovers. The concert offerings range from chamber music to opera, dance, jazz and world-class contemporary performers. The festival was inspired by Richard Wagner and Edvard Grieg, the 19th-century composers who were moved by the natural beauty, gardens and panoramic views of Ravello. For the most part, concerts and events take place at Villa Rufolo and the Auditorium Oscar Niemeyer.

TOP 10 ⭐ Paestum

Paestum enjoyed 1,000 years of prosperity, first as Greek Poseidonia, founded in the 7th century BC, then under the Lucanians, then the Romans. But the crumbling of the Roman Empire led to the gradual abandonment of the city and with that, the degradation of the fields, which turned into malaria-ridden swamps. No one dared come near the spot until the 18th century when Charles III of Spain was having a road built; trees were cut down, and there they were – three intact Greek temples. Much more was discovered in the 20th century.

1 Walls
At its peak, Paestum was large and prosperous, as evidenced by its impressive 5 km (3 miles) of walls, set off with towers and gates at strategic points.

2 Basilica
The oldest temple on the grounds, from c. 530 BC, was most likely dedicated to two deities, Hera and Zeus.

4 Amphitheatre
This Roman structure dates from the 1st century BC or later, and is only partially excavated, the rest lying under the 18th-century road, but some of the exposed part has been rebuilt. Its capacity was small – only about 2,000 – compared to others in the region.

5 Temple of "Ceres"
Votive offerings found here suggest that this small temple, further north than the other sites, was actually dedicated to Athena.

3 Temple of "Neptune"
The last of the three temples to be built at Paestum, in about 450 BC, is also the finest and the best preserved **(above)**. It may have been dedicated to Neptune (Poseidon), but some scholars argue for Apollo, and others for Zeus.

6 Museum
This informative museum exhibits finds from this excavation and several important ones nearby **(left)**. One of those sites is the Sanctuary of Hera Argiva, built by the Greeks at the mouth of the River Sele in about 600 BC. There is a collection of Roman finds upstairs.

7 Tomb Frescoes
Most famous of the exhibits in the museum are the tomb frescoes **(above)**. Virtually the only examples of ancient Greek painting to survive, they are full of light and bright colours.

8 Sculpture
Prime examples in this category of the museum include archaic metopes (decorative architectural elements) and one of two dancing girls from the Sanctuary of Hera Argiva, so well carved in bas-relief that each of the figures seems to be moving in space.

9 Pottery
Fine examples of Grecian urns are on view, including a krater with red-figured painting on black, depicting a young satyr and a girl reluctant to succumb to his blandishments, and an amphora with black figures on red celebrating the fruit of the vine.

10 Artifacts
Other artifacts here include a bronze vase that contained honey, amazingly still liquid at the time it was found due to unique atmospheric conditions below ground.

Map of Paestum

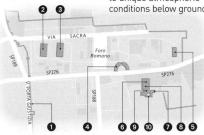

MAGNA GRAECIA

Being great seafarers, the ancient Greeks were indefatigable colonizers. Each important city-state sent out expeditions all over the Mediterranean to set up new cities. Magna Graecia (Greater Greece) formed the southern part of the Italian peninsula, along with Sicily, which the Greeks dominated for centuries, until the Romans expanded their hegemony. Paestum (Poseidonia) was one such Greek city, as were Naples (Neopolis), Cumae, and many more.

NEED TO KNOW

MAP H6 ■ Via Magna Graecia 917 (SS18) ■ www.paestum sites.com

Open 9am–1 hr before sunset daily; museum: 9am–7pm Tue–Sun

Adm €4 for site or museum, €6.50 for both

Tourist Information: Via Magna Graecia 887. 0828 81 10 16/23. www.infopaestum.it

■ Frequent buses run from Salerno to Paestum, and in summer four buses run daily from Naples – call 800 01 66 59 or visit www.cstp.it – or take the train to Paestum Station (1 km/ half a mile from site).

■ There are plenty of quick snacks and light meals available up and down the tourist strip.

■ To see the temples at their most evocative, visit at dawn or at dusk.

The Top 10
of Everything

**Naples' imitation of the Pantheon,
San Francesco di Paola**

Moments in History

1 Greek Colonization

From the 8th to the 5th centuries BC this southern area became an important part of Magna Graecia when Greek city-states set up trading posts here *(see p39)*. In 470 BC Neapolis (New City) was founded, which later became modern Naples.

Norman king, Roger II

2 Vesuvius Erupts

Around 326 BC the area was absorbed into the Roman Empire and by the 1st century AD Naples was a renowned centre of learning. But in August AD 79 all that changed when Mount Vesuvius suddenly erupted after centuries of dormancy. Within a few hours, entire cities were gone, covered by ash or boiling volcanic mud *(see pp30–31)*.

3 Byzantine Siege

With the fall of the Roman Empire in the 5th century, the area was overrun by tribes from the north, particularly the Goths. In 553 the Byzantine emperor Justinian's chief general Belisarius conquered the zone.

4 Norman Conquest

In 1140 the Norman king Roger II made his triumphant entry into Naples – the Normans had already gained possession of Sicily and most of southern Italy. The once proudly autonomous city now had to take a back seat to Palermo – although wellbeing continued to rise, due to the Normans' stability and efficiency.

5 Angevin Capital

In the mid-13th century, the French Anjou dynasty, having taken over the Kingdom of Sicily, shifted its capital to Naples. Many new buildings were erected, including, in 1279, the Castel Nuovo *(see pp14–15)*.

6 Sicilian Vespers

With the removal of the capital to the mainland, Sicilian resentment came to a head on Easter Monday 1282. A riot, known as the Sicilian Vespers, left 2,000 Frenchmen dead and initiated a 20-year war. Finally, Sicily was lost and the Angevin kings focused their attention on Naples, leading to great prosperity.

Sicilian Vespers riot

Giving thanks after the plague

7 Plague of 1656

At the beginning of the 17th century Naples was Europe's largest city, but in 1656 a plague struck. After six months, three-quarters of the people were buried in mass graves.

8 King Charles III Enters in Triumph

In 1734 the Spanish king arrived in Naples. He was heir to the Farnese clan, who were Italian by birth, and transformed his new home town into a city of the Enlightenment.

Garibaldi's arrival in Naples

9 Naples Joins a Unified Italy

On 21 October 1860 Naples voted to join a united Italy, under the rulership of an Italian king, Vittorio Emanuele II – Garibaldi had entered the city two months previously to gather support.

10 Le Quattro Giornate Napoletane

On 27–30 September 1943 Neapolitans showed their true character. After the occupying Nazis threatened to deport all the city's young males, rioting by the populace kept the Germans so busy that the Allies were able to get a toehold and rout the enemy.

TOP 10 HISTORIC FIGURES

1 Parthenope
The siren spurned by Ulysses gave her name to the first Greek colony, in 680 BC, now Pizzofalcone.

2 Spartacus
This runaway slave led a revolt of the oppressed from headquarters on Vesuvius.

3 Romulus Augustulus
The last emperor of the Western Empire died in Naples in AD 476.

4 Belisarius
The general was sent by the Byzantine Emperor to reconquer much of the Italian peninsula in the 5th century.

5 Pope Innocent II
When the Normans were making progress towards Naples in 1137 the city turned to the pope for help, but the Normans took him prisoner.

6 Queen Joan I
Joan (1343–81) was so loved by the people that they forgave her for plotting the murder of her husband.

7 Tommaso Aniello
This fisherman led a revolt in 1647 against the taxation policies of the Spanish rulers.

8 Maria Carolina of Austria
The sister of Marie Antoinette was the power behind the throne of her husband, Ferdinand IV (1768–1811).

9 King Joachim Murat
Napoleon's brother-in-law ascended the throne of Naples in 1808 but was executed in 1815.

10 Antonio Bassolino
Naples' left-wing mayor from 1993 to 2001 brought about a long-overdue clean up of the city.

Maria Carolina of Austria

Artists and their Masterpieces

Crucifixion (c.1308) by Pietro Cavallini

① Pietro Cavallini

Many scholars now credit this Roman artist (c.1259–c.1330) with much of the St Francis fresco in Assisi, formerly attributed to Giotto. Cavallini's work in Naples includes *Scenes from the Lives of Christ and John the Baptist* in San Domenico Maggiore (see p80).

② Donatello

The *bas-relief* of the Assumption, the cardinal's head and the caryatid on the Right of the Tomb of Cardinal Rinaldo Brancaccio in Sant'Angelo a Nilo church (see p80) are assumed to be the only pieces that exist in Naples by this Florentine master (1386–1466).

③ Masaccio

A 15th-century *Crucifixion* by this Tuscan painter (1401–28) is one of the treasures of the Capodimonte Museum. The work is a blend of the formal medieval tradition and the vitality of the Renaissance. Of note are the anatomical accuracy of Christ's torso and the sense of drama created by the outstretched arms of Mary Magdalene.

④ Sandro Botticelli

Typical of this much-loved Florentine artist (1445–1510) is his *Madonna with Child and Two Angels* in the Capodimonte Museum. Although it is an early work, all of the hallmarks of the painter at his height are here: the delicacy of the veils; the refinement of features; and the soulful eyes, evoking sublimity.

⑤ Titian

This consummate painter of the Venetian Renaissance (c.1448–1576) is represented in Naples by several works, all but one in the Capodimonte Museum. These include his sensuous masterpiece *Danaë*, and the religious works *La Maddalena* and *Annunciazione*.

⑥ Caravaggio

This Baroque master (1571–1610) created a lasting artistic revolution with his dramatic use of light and shade. He spent a year or so in Naples; among the works he completed here is *Flagellation of Christ*, originally in San Domenico Maggiore but now in Capodimonte.

Madonna with Child and Two Angels (c.1465) by Sandro Botticelli

7 Domenichino

A mammoth fresco cycle by this painter (1581–1641) adorns the Duomo's Cappella di San Gennaro *(see p16)*, depicting episodes from the life of Naples' patron saint.

8 Jusepe Ribera

The Spanish painter (1590–1652) spent much of his life in Naples, where he created powerful and original works. These include his *San Sebastiano* in the Certosa di San Martino *(see p28)*.

9 Artemisia Gentileschi

It is said that Gentileschi (1593–1652) was violated in her youth and brought the pain of her indignation to her astounding *Judith and Holofernes*, now in Capodimonte. She was virtually the only female artist of the age to rise to fame.

Triumph of Judith by Luca Giordano

10 Luca Giordano

One of the most prolific of Naples' Baroque artists (1634–1705). His paintings and frescoes are ubiquitous in the city, adorning churches and museums. Most significant is *Triumph of Judith* (1704) on the Treasury ceiling in the Certosa di San Martino *(see pp26–9)*.

TOP 10 WRITERS AND PHILOSOPHERS

St Thomas Aquinas

1 Virgil
The epic poet (70–19 BC) lived in Naples for many years, incorporating local legends into his work *The Aeneid*.

2 Petronius
In his saga *The Satyricon* (only a fragment survives), this author (d. AD 66) captures the decadence of the Roman Empire in the villas of Naples.

3 Pliny the Younger
Thanks to this writer (AD 62–113) we know much about the day Vesuvius erupted and buried Pompeii *(see p33)*.

4 Suetonius
The writer (AD 70–126) is famous for his *Twelve Caesars*, scandalous accounts of the first Roman emperors.

5 St Thomas Aquinas
The theologian (1225–74) was often a guest at San Domenico Maggiore, headquarters for religious study at the University of Naples.

6 Petrarch
The great lyric poet and scholar (1313–74) often visited the court of Robert of Anjou in Naples.

7 Giovanni Boccaccio
Author of *The Decameron* (1348–53), 10 tales of ribaldry in medieval Naples.

8 Torquato Tasso
Tasso was an epic poet and a native of Sorrento (1544–95).

9 Giovanni Battista Vico
Born in Naples, Vico (1668–1744) found fame with his influential *La Scienza Nuova (The New Science)* published in 1725.

10 Benedetto Croce
The philosopher, historian and statesman (1866–1952) spent much time in Naples.

TOP 10 Icons of Popular Culture

Pulcinella figurines, Naples

1 Pulcinella

Cunning, perpetually hungry and rambunctious, Pulcinella (Little Chicken) is the symbol of Neapolitans and their streetwise way of life. His signature white pyjama-like outfit, peaked hat and hook-nosed mask go back to ancient Roman burlesque, in which a bawdy clown, Macchus, was one of the stock characters. He is the prototype of Punch and similar anarchic puppets around the world.

2 Presepi

The tradition of creating sculpted tableaux of Christ's birth (presepi) has risen to a high art in Naples ever since the 1700s. Many sculptors create scenes that expand far beyond the central event and include features of everyday life – Pulcinella might be represented slapping the current mayor, for example.

3 Sophia Loren

An indefatigable love goddess since her star began to rise in 1957 in L'Oro di Napoli (The Gold of Naples), "La Loren" went on to become a Hollywood star.

Sophia Loren

4 Scugnizzi and Lazzaroni

These two characters, products of the poverty the city has historically suffered, are street urchins and ruffians. Both have been heavily romanticized by outsiders, yet their sly wisdom and wit are traits all Neapolitans seem to aspire to.

5 Neapolitan Song

Naples has always been known as a city of music, with songs focusing nostalgically on love, the sun and the sea. O' Sole Mio and Santa Lucia are the most renowned.

Un Turco Napoletano, starring Totò

6 Totò

This rubber-faced comedian was the quintessence of Italian humour. Until his death in 1967, "The Prince of Laughter" made five films a year, some of them comic master-pieces, including Un Turco Napoletano (A Neapolitan Turk, 1953).

7 Pino Daniele

Known as the voice of Naples, Pino Daniele was one of Italy's most popular singer-songwriters. He was known abroad for his songs Quando and Je so pazz. After his death, a street in Naples was named in his honour.

8 Massimo Troisi

Embodying the heart of the Neapolitan character, this actor made international waves with *Il Postino (The Postman)*, nominated for an Academy Award in 1995. Sadly, after the film was completed, Troisi died at the age of 41.

Massimo Troisi

9 Naples in the Movies

Greats of the golden age of Italian cinema all felt inspired to communicate their impressions of Naples. Notable films include Roberto Rossellini's *Viaggio in Italia* (1954) and Francesco Rossi's *Mani Sulla Città* (1963).

10 Recent International Films

Naples and the coast have provided the setting for films as diverse as the fifth *Star Wars* instalment, which used the Royal Palace at Caserta for the queen's abode, and Anthony Minghella's *The Talented Mr Ripley*, some scenes of which were shot on the islands of Procida and Ischia.

A scene from *The Talented Mr Ripley*

TOP 10 OPERA LEGENDS

Gaetano Donizetti

1 Teatro San Carlo
The oldest continuously working opera theatre in Europe is a UNESCO World Heritage site *(see p89)*.

2 Inauguration
On 4 November 1737 the San Carlo was inaugurated with Metastasio's opera *Achille in Sciro*.

3 Castrati
An 18th-century Neapolitan speciality, renowned *castrati* included Farinelli (Carlo Broschi) and Gian Battista Velluti.

4 Fire
A February 1816 fire destroyed the San Carlo. In a few months the theatre had been rebuilt with perfect acoustics.

5 Ballet
San Carlo shares with La Scala the record for the first Italian ballet school (1812).

6 Gioacchino Rossini
The composer was artistic director of the opera house between 1815 and 1822.

7 Gaetano Donizetti
Donizetti composed 16 operas for the San Carlo.

8 Vincenzo Bellini
In 1826 Bellini staged his first work at the San Carlo, *Bianca e Gerlando*.

9 Giuseppe Verdi
The "god" of Italian opera wrote his first opera for the theatre, *Alzira*, in 1845.

10 Enrico Caruso
Arguably the most famous tenor ever, Caruso was born in Naples in 1873.

🔟 Museums and Galleries

18th-century Nativity scene, Museo di San Martino, Naples

1 Museo di San Martino, Naples

This monastery complex is home to several collections of art. The Pinacoteca, comprising part of the Prior's Quarters, is notable for its works from the Renaissance and Baroque eras, many commissioned for the monastery. On the upper floors, 19th-century works convey the look and feel of Naples in the days of Italian Unification. A section devoted to Nativity scenes demonstrates the power and beauty of this Neapolitan art form *(see pp26–9)*.

2 Museobottega della Tarsialignea, Sorrento

MAP D5 ▪ Via S Nicola 28 ▪ 081 877 19 42 ▪ Open Apr–Oct: 10am–6:30pm daily; Nov–Mar: 10am–5pm daily ▪ Adm

Sorrento is known for its fine inlaid wood furniture and objects *(intarsio)* and this museum is devoted to the delicate art. The collection is housed in a beautiful restored palace.

Inlaid wood desk at the Museobottega della Tarsialignea

3 Museo Archeologico, Naples

An insurpassable museum for the range and beauty of its Greco-Roman art, with important pieces unearthed in Rome and in towns around Vesuvius. The experience is a total immersion in the life of the ancients – their religious beliefs, sports, eating habits, and even their erotic peccadilloes *(see pp18–21)*.

4 Capodimonte, Naples

This world-class museum also owes its main masterpieces to the Farnese Collection. Paintings run the gamut from medieval to contemporary; the porcelain collection also shouldn't be missed *(see pp22–3)*.

5 Pinacoteca Girolamini, Naples

MAP P2 ▪ Via Duomo 142 ▪ Open 9am–12:30pm Mon–Sat

For Neapolitan Baroque lovers, this little-known gallery is a must. Part of a monastic complex, there are fine works by Caracciolo, Vaccaro, Giordano and Ribera.

6 Museo Nazionale della Ceramica Duca di Martina, Naples

MAP J4 ■ Via Cimarosa 77
■ Open 8:30am–2pm; closed Tue
■ Adm ■ DA ■ www.coopculture.it

Naples is famous for fine ceramic production and this museum provides rich amplification of the theme. Not only are exquisite Italian pieces found here, by Capodimonte and Ginori artisans, but also there are creations by the factories of Meissen, Limoges, Sèvres and Saint-Cloud. Majolica works, from medieval times onwards, are also well represented, and the collection of Chinese and Japanese ceramics, from as far back as the T'ang Dynasty, is one of the country's best.

Museo Archeologico di Pithecusae figurine

7 Museo della Carta, Amalfi

This fascinating museum, which is set in a paper mill, preserves one of Europe's first papermaking factories. Visitors can see the original stone vats and machinery downstairs, and there's also an interesting exhibit tracing the history and technical development of the paper industry over the centuries (see p36).

8 Museo Diego Aragona Pignatelli Cortes, Naples

MAP K6 ■ Riviera di Chiaia 200
■ Open 8:30am–7pm Wed–Mon ■ Adm

The striking Neo-Classical Villa Pignatelli was built in 1826 by Pietro Valente for the Acton family. The Rothschilds acquired the villa 20 years later, then Prince Diego Aragona Pignatelli Cortes bought it and renamed the house. In 1952 his granddaughter donated it to the Italian state. The loveliest rooms are the red hall furnished in Louis XVI style, the smoking room with leather-lined walls and the ballroom with its large mirrors and magnificent chandeliers. Also of particular interest is the Coach Museum. Today, the Villa Pignatelli often plays host to temporary exhibitions and concerts.

9 Museo Archeologico di Pithecusae, Ischia

MAP A4 ■ Corso Angelo Rizzoli 210, Lacco Ameno ■ 081 99 61 03
■ Open 9:30am–1:30pm; closed Mon
■ Adm

Housed in the 18th-century Villa Arbusto, exhibits illustrate the history of ancient Ischia, from prehistoric to Roman times. Many objects date back to the 8th century BC, when Ischia was settled by Greeks. The most famous pots were found at a nearby necropolis; among these are a typical late geometric *krater*, decorated with a shipwreck scene.

10 Museo Archeologico, Paestum

Among this museum's beautiful treasures are ancient Greek tomb paintings that were only discovered on the site in 1968. Other finds include bronze vases, terracotta votive figures and various funerary furnishings (see pp38–39).

Tomb painting, Museo Archeologico, Paestum

Churches in Naples

Santa Chiara's majolica cloister

1 Santa Chiara
The original church here was built in 1310 and, after various renovations, it has been returned to its glorious Gothic style. The most famous feature is the adjoining convent's 18th-century majolica cloister *(see p77)*.

2 San Francesco di Paola
A rarity in Naples, this Neo-Classical structure imitates the Pantheon, Rome's great pagan temple to the gods built in the 2nd century AD. Inside and out the basilica is austere, with the exception of the polychrome marble Baroque altar that has many statues *(see p87)*.

3 Duomo
The oldest wing of Naples' cathedral is the city's most ancient surviving building, a Paleo-Christian church dating from the 4th century. The cathedral also has the oldest baptistry in the western world, with glorious mosaics. Archaeological excavations here have revealed structures reaching as far back as the ancient Greeks *(see pp16–17)*.

4 Monte di Pietà
MAP P2 ▪ Via S Biagio 114
▪ Open 9am–7pm Sat (to 2pm Sun)
This majestic building and its adjoining church were built in the late 1500s as a charitable institute set up to grant loans to the needy. In return, the noblemen who provided this service were granted eternal salvation. Decorated mostly in late-Renaissance style, inside there are sculptures by Pietro Bernini and frescoes by Corenzio.

5 Santa Maria Maggiore
MAP N2 ▪ Via dei Tribunali
▪ Open 9am–1pm Mon–Sat (adjacent chapel only)
Nicknamed *Pietrasanta* (holy stone) after its ancient stone marked with a cross, thought to grant indulgences to whoever kissed it, the original church here was built in the 10th and 11th centuries and the bell tower is Naples' only example of early medieval architecture. The present church, however, is Baroque.

San Francesco di Paola, dominating Piazza del Plebiscito

6 Pio Monte della Misericordia

MAP Q2 ■ Via dei Tribunali 253 ■ 081 44 69 44/73 ■ Open 9am–2pm Thu–Tue

This charitable institution was founded in 1601, inspired by Counter-Reformation precepts which gave weight to such works as a way of ensuring salvation. The church is set back from the street by a five-arch loggia, where pilgrims could find shelter. The altarpiece, *The Seven Acts of Mercy* by Caravaggio, is an allegory of charitable deeds. Upstairs is an art collection.

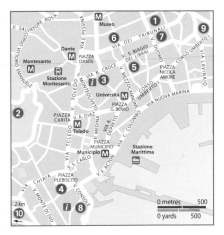

Ceiling fresco, Certosa di San Martino

7 Certosa di San Martino

This sparkling white monastery complex commands the most perfect location in the entire city, attesting to the wealth and power the monks once enjoyed. In the 17th and 18th centuries they commissioned the greatest artists of the day to embellish their church and chambers in Baroque style – the church, in particular, is a flamboyant catalogue of colour and pattern, sporting at least one work by each and every famous hand of the age (see pp26–7).

8 Santa Lucia

MAP N6 ■ Via Sta Lucia 3 ■ 081 764 09 43 ■ Open 8am–noon, 5–7:30pm daily

According to legend, a church stood here in ancient times, but experts date the earliest structure to the 9th century. Destroyed and rebuilt many times, the present church is postwar. The artworks were destroyed during World War II, save an 18th-century statue of St Lucy and two paintings.

9 San Pietro ad Aram

MAP R2 ■ Corso Umberto I 192 ■ Open 8am–noon, 4–6:30pm Mon–Fri; 8am–noon Sun

Tradition holds that St Peter celebrated his first mass in Naples here. The church is 12th-century, but an early Christian church and catacombs were unearthed in 1930.

10 Santa Maria del Parto

MAP J2 ■ Via Mergellina 21 ■ Open 4:30–8pm daily

The Neapolitan poet (and humanist) Jacopo Sannazaro, ordered this church to be built in the 16th century and his tomb behind the high altar is notable for its lack of Christian symbolism. In a side chapel the painting of the Archangel Michael searing the "Mergellina Devil" records the spiritual victory of a bishop when a woman proclaimed her love for him.

Piazzas and Fountains

1 Piazza Plebiscito, Naples

MAP M5

This vast, magnificent urban space has been restored to its original grandeur. On one side is the church of San Francesco di Paola (see p87), and on the other the Palazzo Reale (see pp12–13). The royal equestrian statues on the square are all the work of Canova.

Fontana dell' Immacolatella

2 Fontana dell' Immacolatella, Naples

MAP K2 ■ **Via Partenope, near Castel dell'Ovo**

Composed of three triumphal arches, this Santa Lucia district landmark once adorned the Palazzo Reale. It dates from 1601 and is another creation of Pietro Bernini, as well as Michelangelo Naccherino. This grand fountain stands at one end of the seafront Lungomare

(see p54), while the Sebeto Fountain, a later work by Cosimo Fanzago, marks the other terminus.

3 Fontana del Nettuno, Naples

MAP P4

Shifted from its home at Piazza Bovio in 2001, the beautiful Fountain of Neptune now graces a wide spot on Via Medina. The 16th-century masterpiece is the work of three artists, including Pietro Bernini.

4 Piazza Bellini, Naples

Without a doubt, this is central Naples' most charming square. With inviting café tables lined up on the sunny side and elegant architecture facing all around, Piazza Bellini is a favourite spot for intellectuals, artists, students and anyone who wants to take a break (see p79).

5 Piazza Dante, Naples

MAP N2

Following Italian Unification, a statue of the poet Dante was placed in the centre of the broad curve of this square, which was accordingly renamed. Before that, the area was known as Largo del Mercatello, when it was a major marketplace. Today it is still a busy focal point of the old part of the city.

Dante's statue, Piazza Dante

6 Piazza Sannazzaro, Naples
MAP K2

The nautical theme of the mermaid and turtles fountain is appropriate, as the nearby port is the main one for embarking on a trip to the islands of Capri, Ischia or Procida.

7 Piazza Duomo, Ravello
MAP E4

A visit to Ravello should begin in this charming piazza, as there are a number of different routes you can take from here. Staircases and ramped walkways lead off in all directions.

8 La Piazzetta, Capri

Magnetic at any time, this is Capri's most frequented spot. Marked by a domed bell tower, it has many cafés with tables outside, surrounded by whitewashed arcades (see pp34–5).

La Piazzetta, Capri

9 Piazza Tasso, Sorrento
MAP D5

The bustling heart of Sorrento, this piazza is the focal point of daily life. Find a spot at a café surrounding the square to take it all in. Constructed over a deep ravine, the square is named after the 16th-century poet Torquato Tasso from Sorrento. From the piazza, a steep road leads down to Marina Piccola, where ferries arrive and depart.

10 Piazza Duomo, Amalfi
MAP E5

Dominated by the steps up to the cathedral and the black-and-white design of the building and its bell tower, this square is a hub of café life.

TOP 10 PARKS AND GARDENS

Gardens of Augustus, Capri

1 Santi Marcellino e Festo Cloister, Naples
MAP P3 ▪ Largo S Marcellino 10 ▪ Open 8am–8pm Mon–Fri, 8am–2pm Sat
The site of former 8th-century monasteries enjoys fine views.

2 Orto Botanico, Naples
The "Royal Plant Garden" was founded by Joseph Bonaparte in 1807 (see p79).

3 Capodimonte, Naples
Established by Charles III, this vast royal park boasts numerous ancient trees (see pp22–3).

4 Villa La Floridiana, Naples
These grounds have been a public park since the 1920s (see p60).

5 Villa Comunale, Naples
This large public park is now appreciated for its statuary and fine structures (see p88).

6 Parco Virgiliano, Naples
This hilltop position provides fine panoramas (see p111).

7 Caserta Park, Naples
These 18th-century gardens were influenced by Versailles (see p113).

8 La Mortella, Ischia
MAP A4 ▪ Via F Calise 39, Forio ▪ Open Mar–Nov: 9am–7pm Tue–Thu, Sat–Sun ▪ Adm
Ischia's fabulous gardens include rare species.

9 Gardens of Augustus, Capri
MAP C5 ▪ Via Matteotti ▪ Open dawn–dusk daily ▪ Adm
The island's primary green spot.

10 Villa Cimbrone, Ravello
Many agree that the view from Villa Cimbrone is the most beautiful in the world (see p37).

 Walks

Wonderful landscape for walking on Capri

① Decumano Maggiore
MAP P2

In Roman times this street, now known as Via dei Tribunali, was the main east–west artery of the city. Decumano Maggiore constitutes the heart of the old quarter and is replete with unmissable sights, as well as intriguing shops and bars and cafés to while away the hours.

② Royal Naples
MAP P4

For regal edifices and elegant cafés and shops, this choice part of town is pedestrian-friendly. A good place to start is the Fontana del Nettuno on Via Medina (see p50) and then head towards the sea and west. This arc takes in Castel Nuovo, Teatro San Carlo and Galleria Umberto I.

Castel Nuovo, Naples

③ Capri

Once you break away from the smart shops and hotels, this island is all about nature walks: up to Villa Jovis, down to the Arco Naturale, through the forest to the Blue Grotto – the possibilities are numerous (see pp34–5).

④ Spaccanapoli

The colloquial name of this ancient street means "Splits Naples", which is exactly what it does, cutting the oldest part of the city right down the middle. Beginning at the western end in Piazza del Gesù Nuovo, a straight line takes you past some of the city's finest monuments, and there are shops, bars, cafés and pizzerias (see pp76–85).

⑤ Lungomare
MAP N6

Beginning at the public gardens next to the Palazzo Reale, take the seaside road around the Santa Lucia quarter and past some of Naples' loveliest areas, including the island of Castel dell'Ovo and the green splendour of the Villa Comunale.

⑥ Via Toledo
MAP N3

From the royal quarter Via Toledo begins elegantly, but soon the

Quartieri Spagnoli (Spanish Quarters) come up along the western flank – a warren of narrow, dark streets that don't seem to have changed in centuries. However, continuing on you'll pass Piazza Dante and finally come to the Museo Archeologico.

7 Sorrentine Peninsula
MAP D5

If you take the *funivia* (cable car) from Castellammare di Stabia up to Monte Faito there are startling views from the top, as well as the beginning of many nature trails, some of which eventually lead as far as Positano.

8 The Amalfi Coast

Hiking points can be reached above Positano and between Ravello and Amalfi-Atrani. Most of these paths are erstwhile goat trails – the most famous is the *Sentieri degli Dei* (Path of the Gods) – while some have been built up as stone stairways; all offer incomparable views *(see p103)*.

Walking the rim of Mount Vesuvius

9 Vesuvius

A walk along the rim of this vast crater is an experience of a life-time. Some 20,000 visitors a year trek to the top to peer into the steaming depths 200 m (700 ft) below. The steep hike up takes about 30 minutes and it's at its best in late spring, when flowers are most vibrant *(see p95)*.

10 Ischia

The walks and hikes on this island are plentiful. A memorable trek is up Monte Epomeo from Forio, through Fontana, taking about 40 minutes *(see p101)*.

TOP 10 DRIVES

Vietri from above

1 The Phlegrean Fields
MAP J2
Hug the coastline from Posillipo to Pozzuoli and take local roads to Agnano Terme and La Solfatara.

2 Cumae
MAP B3
Begin at Lago d'Averno and pass under the Arco Felice to arrive at Cumae.

3 Naples to Sorrento
MAP E4
Cut off the tollway to Castellammare di Stabia and take the picturesque road.

4 Sorrento to Positano
MAP D5
Follow the signs to Santa Agata sui Due Golfi and then Colli di Fontanelle to get your first glimpse of Positano.

5 Positano to Vietri
MAP E5
A single road "of 1,000 turns" winds along this spectacular coast.

6 Amalfi to Ravello
MAP E5
Leave the coast road and climb up and up for a vista unlike any other.

7 Around Ischia
MAP B4
A fairly good road rings the island.

8 Marina Grande to Anacapri, Capri
MAP S1
The cliff road is best experienced in the island's classic open-top taxis.

9 Naples to Caserta
MAP D1
Getting up to this northern palace is well worth the effort.

10 Naples to Paestum
MAP H6
Take the A3, then switch to the N19, direction Battipaglia. Take the right fork for Paestum, the N18 south.

Following pages Santa Maria Assunta Church, Positano

🔟 Beaches

One of many beaches on Procida

1 Procida

This small island has several good beach options. One of the longest stretches from Chiaiolella Marina to Ciriaccio, called the Lido, is the island's most popular beach so expect crowds. From here a bridge leads to the nature reserve of Vivara, which has rocky access to the sea. To the northeast, Pozzo Vecchio also has a beach (see p102).

2 Posillipo and Beyond
MAP J2

The nearest beaches to the centre of Naples that are of any appeal can be found at Posillipo, although they're shingle, not sand, and the water is far from immaculate. Further away, at the ends of the Cumana and Circumflegrea railways, there are more attractive sandy beaches, although, again, they are not especially pristine.

3 Sorrento

In this resort town, bathing platforms have been constructed, with lifts or steps leading down to them from several

hotels, but unless you are a hotel resident you will have to pay for this option. Elsewhere along the peninsula there's a fine beach to the east, at Meta di Sorrento, while to the west, there's a small sandy beach at Marina di Puolo and another at Marina di Lobra (see p102).

4 Capri

There's very little in the way of sandy beaches here, although there is a small one just up from Marina Grande. A popular pebbly choice is Marina Piccola, where facilities include restaurants. The adventurous should head down to the bottom of Via Krupp, where huge flat stones lie along the shore (see pp34–5).

View over the bay, Capri

5 Ischia

To gain access to any beach here – at least the good parts – you will need to pay, but for around €15 to €20 per day you receive the use of a sunbed and an umbrella. There are plenty of beaches to choose from, including sandy stretches in Forio and Ischia Porto. More out-of-the-way options include San Montano and Sorgeto (see p101).

Pretty Ischia beach

Marina Grande beach, Amalfi

6 Amalfi

Lined with colourful umbrellas, the Marina Grande beach has a free area popular with locals. Or take a short boat ride to the rocky Santa Croce beach (see p104).

7 Positano

Again, at this fashionable, busy resort, payment is necessary for a sunbed and umbrella. For something more independent take the path to the west, around the cliff, to the beach at Fornillo – it's smaller and rockier but more relaxed (see p104).

8 Marina di Praia

This small cove, just beyond Positano, has a bit of beach you can generally call your own, as few tourists stop here. However you will share the cove with local fishing boats, a couple of bar-restaurants, a diving centre and the coast's premier disco, Africana (see p107).

9 Marina di Furore

MAP E5

A very precipitous path goes straight down to this dramatic, tiny beach set between the cliffs. A few fishermen's homes cluster here, with their boats neatly moored along one side, and there's a bar-restaurant.

10 Erchie and Cetara

MAP F4

The beach at Erchie is a small cove graced by a watchtower, fishing boats and a few houses. At Cetara, bathers share the narrow rocky strip with boats, but it's good for a dip.

Parco Termale Aphrodite Apollon

🔟 Romantic Spots

Terrace of Infinity, Villa Cimbrone

an excellent place for a peaceful stroll, and the main building now houses a museum filled with a number of delightful treasures *(see p53)*.

3 Ristorante Da Adolfo, Positano
MAP E5 ■ Via Laurito 40 ■ 089 87 50 22 ■ €€€

Hidden away in a tiny cove just east of Positano is the tranquil Laurito beach. Since 1966, this beachside restaurant has been serving freshly caught fish, mozzarella grilled on lemon leaves, and locally made wine with fresh peaches. The restaurant offers a free boat service for clients from Positano's main pier and the ride is five minutes. Sunbeds and umbrellas are available to rent, so arrive early for a romantic day at the beach.

1 Villa Cimbrone, Ravello
Greta Garbo enjoyed her love affair with the conductor Arturo Toscanini in this lovely spot, declared by American writer Gore Vidal to be one of the most beautiful places on earth. Wander the maze-like gardens over terraced levels; the highlight is the Terrace of Infinity, with breathtaking views *(see p36)*.

2 Villa La Floridiana, Naples
MAP J4 ■ Via Domenico Cimarosa 77 ■ Open 8:30am–2pm (to 7pm in summer)

Lucia Migliaccio, Duchess of Floridia, once called this sumptuous place home – a love token from her husband, Ferdinand I, whose morganatic wife she became soon after the death of his first wife, Maria Carolina of Austria. Not only is the story romantic but the situation itself affords some of the finest views of the city and the bay. The gardens are

4 Le Sirenuse, Positano
In the heart of Positano, Le Sirenuse has earned its reputation as one of the most romantic hotels on the Amalfi Coast. Even if you're not a guest, you can enjoy an unforgettable meal with a view at the Michelin-starred La Sponda restaurant *(see p131)*.

Balcony at Le Sirenuse, Positano

Coastline at Marechiaro

5 Marechiaro

This little fishing village between the tip of Capo di Posillipo and Punta del Cavallo is famous with locals for its time-tested romantic atmosphere. The vista from here is said to be so gorgeous that even the fish come here to woo their sweethearts, especially by the light of the moon. There are many excellent and inviting restaurants clustered around the prime viewing spot, all specializing in fish, of course (see p111).

6 Monastero Santa Rosa, Conca dei Marini

MAP E5 ▪ Via Roma 2 ▪ 089 832 11 99
With a secluded setting, this former monastery is the dream hotel for a romantic escape on the Amalfi Coast. Wander hand in hand through the terraced gardens or enjoy a dip in the beautiful infinity pool (see p130).

7 Le Grottelle Restaurant, Capri

MAP U1 ▪ Via Arco Naturale ▪ 081 837 57 19 ▪ Closed mid-Nov–Mar, Tue (not Jul–Aug) ▪ €€
The cuisine here is simple, homemade fare that includes seafood, pasta, chicken and perhaps rabbit, while the wine is local and very creditable. What makes it so romantic is the unsurpassed setting. Not only is it close to nature, being situated almost all the way down to the Arco Naturale, but the terrace tables also enjoy an eye-popping view straight down to the sea, along a precipitous ravine. In addition, the friendly owners do their best to make any meal a memorable event.

8 Villa Eva Resort, Anacapri

Set amid subtropical gardens, this resort consists of a main house and bungalows. Each accommodation is unique and there's a wonderful grand piano-shaped pool (see p128).

9 Garden of Augustus, Capri

Capri is an island of romance, but the views from the Gardens of Augustus makes it one of the most romantic spots. The gardens are perfect for admiring the Faraglioni rocks, zigzagging Via Krupp and mesmerizing turquoise sea (see p35).

Garden of Augustus, Capri

10 Villa Maria Restaurant, Ravello

MAP E4 ▪ Via Sta Chiara 2 ▪ 089 85 72 55 ▪ DA ▪ €€
Such a beautiful view from the vine-covered garden deserves superb food, and that is just what you find here. The restaurant, part of the Hotel Villa Maria (see p130), is one of Ravello's best, specializing in fresh fish and seafood as well as local wines; try the incredible lemon mousse.

For a key to restaurant price ranges see p85

Off the Beaten Track

① Green Grotto, Capri
MAP U2

On the other side of the island from its far more famous sibling, the Blue Grotto *(see p35)*, this smaller cave glows emerald green once you duck inside. The best way to get here is to rent a kayak at Punta Carena and then make your way past Marina Piccola towards the Faraglioni rocks.

Green Grotto entrance, Capri

② Napoli Sotterranea
MAP P2 ■ Piazza S Gaetano 68 ■ 081 40 02 56 ■ Guided tours in English: 10am, noon, 2pm, 4pm and 6pm ■ Adm

This tour's entrance is next to San Paolo Maggiore *(see p80)* and takes you into a world of excavations that date back to the 4th century BC (bring a jacket as it can be cool). The digging began when the Greeks quarried large tufa blocks to build the city of Neapolis. Caves were also dug here to be used as tombs. Centuries later the Romans turned this underground area into aqueducts and cisterns, which were in use until the cholera epidemic of 1884.

③ San Gaudioso Catacombs
MAP K1 ■ Basilica of Sta Maria della Sanità, Via della Sanità 124 ■ Guided tours: every hour between 10am and 1pm ■ Adm

This labyrinth of underground tunnels was built by the Romans for use as cisterns. It evolved into catacombs in the 5th century, when St Gaudiosus, a North African bishop and hermit, was interred here. Visitors can see the remains of fresco and mosaic decorations.

④ Spiaggia di Fornillo, Positano

Few know that there's a pleasant alternative to the crowded main beach at Positano, with its rows of sunbeds and umbrellas. To get to Fornillo, head west on the path past the 'O Guarracino restaurant, around the cliff. It's a rocky beach, over-looked by two towers, but there's a café-restaurant and facilities *(see p59)*.

⑤ Cimitero delle Fontanelle
MAP K1 ■ Via delle Fontanelle 154 ■ 081 29 69 44 ■ Open by appt only

Once a Roman quarry for tufa blocks, this cavern became a gruesome depository for the city's dead during the cholera epidemic of 1884. Graves and tombs were emptied all over Naples and the skulls stacked here – some 40,000 in all, with the addition of still more during the cholera outbreak of 1974.

Skulls, Cimitero delle Fontanelle

Colourful galleries, at MADRe

6 MADRe
MAP P1 ■ Via Settembrini 79
■ 081 193 130 16 ■ Open 10am–
7:30pm Wed–Mon (to 8pm Sun) ■ Adm

Housed in a 14th-century church, this museum aims to bring contemporary art to the forefront. Exhibitions from the 1940s onwards contrast with the surrounding history of Naples. Permanent exhibitions include the Historical Collection, exploring artistic language.

7 Sibyl's Grotto, Cumae
Although some experts believe that this magnificent structure once served a military purpose in Roman times, others hold with a mythological origin. Walking along the unusual wedge-shaped walls, which are pierced at intervals with shafts of light, creates a decidedly hypnotic effect on most visitors, as if in preparation for an encounter with the great oracle herself (priestess of Apollo) in her grotto *(see p113)*.

8 Tomb of Virgil and Crypta Neapolitana
MAP K2 ■ Salita della Grotta 20, Mergellina ■ Open 9am–5pm Tue–Sun

What is known as Virgil's tomb is a Roman burial vault that dates back to the Augustan age. It is a typical *columbarium*, the "dovecote" style of burial, with niches for urns containing the ashes of the deceased. The Romans later took to burying their dead in sarcophagi (coffins), as the fashion changed to belief in an afterlife, perhaps adopted from the Egyptians. Next to the tomb are a tufa quarry and a *crypta* (tunnel), built as an underground road in the 1st century.

9 Parco Sommerso, Baia
MAP B3 ■ Glass-bottom boat tours or land tours: call 349 497 41 83 or visit www.baiasommersa.it; diving and snorkelling tours: call 081 853 15 63

Most of the ancient city of Baia now lies underwater, due to the shifting of the coastline and slow seismic disturbances. What you can still make out just below the surface of the water are remnants of the grandiose port and parts of various villas and temples *(see p112)*.

San Gennaro Catacombs

10 San Gennaro Catacombs
MAP K1 ■ Via Capodimonte 13
■ Guided tours: every hour between 10am & 7pm Mon–Sat, between 10am & 1pm Sun and public hols ■ Adm

Burials here date back to the 2nd century and the site was originally used by pagans as well as Christians. In the 5th century, the body of San Gennaro, Naples' patron saint, was brought here, and the place became an important pilgrimage site. Frescoes and mosaics on the two levels of this vast layout attest to its importance over the centuries.

Children's Attractions

1 Villa Comunale
This major urban park in central Naples has a playground specifically designed for little ones and there are always plenty of families enjoying the gardens and walkways. But the biggest attraction for youngsters may be the Stazione Zoologica (Zoological Institute), the oldest aquarium in Europe, featuring sea life from the Bay of Naples *(see p88)*.

2 Science City
A hands-on, interactive "experimentorium", with something for everyone, even the very young. Included in the exhibits are a planetarium (booking ahead is compulsory and incurs an extra fee) as well as up-to-date computer gizmos, all of which seem to transcend language barriers *(see p114)*.

Tyrannosaurus rex skeleton, Centro Musei delle Scienze Naturali

3 Centro Musei delle Scienze Naturali
MAP P3 ■ Via Mezzocannone 8 & Largo S Marcellino 10 ■ 081 253 75 87 ■ Open 9am–1:30pm Mon–Fri (also open 3–5pm Mon & Thu)

The Università di Napoli Federico II houses five museums in one building. Sedimentologists will love the Mineralogy and Geology sections; the Zoology rooms will appeal to animal lovers; the Palaeonotology Museum has dinosaur exhibits; and the Anthropology and Physics areas are extremely fascinating.

Exhibit, Pietrarsa Railway Museum

4 Pietrarsa Railway Museum
MAP D3 ■ Via Pietrarsa, Portici ■ 081 567 23 02 ■ Open 8:30am–12:30pm Mon–Sat ■ Adm

The first railway in Italy was inaugurated by King Ferdinand II in 1839 and 150 years later the railway workshop was opened as a museum. The museum is the largest of its kind in Europe and has impressive displays, including a reconstruction of the first royal train here and a line-up of later carriages, many of them lavishly gilded.

5 Edenlandia
MAP J2 ■ Viale Kennedy, Fuorigrotta ■ 081 239 40 90 ■ Open Jul: 5pm–midnight Tue–Sun (to 10:30pm Sun); Aug: 10:30pm–midnight daily; hours vary rest of the year – phone or check website for details ■ Adm ■ edenlandiapark.it

This traditional amusement park might be showing its age a bit and isn't giving Disney any competition, but kids of all ages will enjoy its attractions. Rides include a Big Dipper, a Ghost Train, a Canoe Flume and Bumper Cars, as well as several more high-tech options. An old-fashioned choice that never fails to delight is Le Nuvole, a theatre group that features puppets and mime.

6 Zoo di Napoli
MAP C3 ▪ Via J F Kennedy 76 ▪ 081 193 631 54 ▪ Open Apr–Oct: 9:30am–7pm; Nov–Mar: 9:30am–5pm ▪ Adm ▪ www.lozoodinapoli.com

Home to 409 different animals, the Naples zoo allows visitors to see and pet them up close and, in some cases, even get in the pens along with the zookeepers. There are also educational activities organized for kids.

7 Solfatara
Another phenomenal geothermal playground that will fascinate budding geologists. This congealed lava cap plugging up a dormant volcano is an expanse of hissing, fuming, bubbling terrain like nothing you will have seen before. There's a camp site with restaurant right on the spot – you soon get used to the sulphur smell (see p114).

8 Marina Piccola Beach, Capri
One of the most child-friendly beaches in the area: the water is tranquil and the bathing areas well protected. For all the water toys and gear you might require, there are lots of shops handy, and a wide choice of places to eat. Changing rooms, umbrellas and sunbeds are available, too (see p34).

Marina Piccola Beach, Capri

9 Ospedale delle Bambole
MAP P2 ▪ Via S Biagio dei Librai 81 ▪ Open 10am–5pm Mon–Fri

Children are captivated by the Doll Hospital, both for the concept as well as for the array of dolls that are here waiting to be "cured". Adults, too, will find this unique workshop fascinating, with some pieces in the collection qualifying as museum-quality treasures. There is also a shop, so your child won't necessarily have to say goodbye to a new-found friend at the end of the visit.

Dolls, Ospedale delle Bambole

10 Vesuvius
No child will ever forget a trip up the cone of this killer volcano and a peek over the rim into the steaming abyss far below. It's a fairly short, steep walk – only about half an hour – and the thrill will stay with them for years (see p95).

Neapolitan Dishes

1 Contorni

The fertility of the land around Naples is most evident when you taste the produce it brings forth. For *contorni* (side dishes), peppers, artichokes, aubergine (eggplant), capers, mushrooms and green beans are offered steamed or sautéed. Expect the freshness to have been retained fully, cooked with a touch of garlic, tomato or lemon, and herbs.

2 Primo

This course usually means pasta or rice, but *minestre* and *zuppe* (soups) also appear in this category. Great *primi* to look out for are *spaghetti alle vongole veraci* (with clams), *pasta e fagioli* (with beans), *fettucine alla puttanesca* (egg noodles with tomato, capers, black olives and red pepper) and *risotto alla pescatora* (rice with seafood).

Insalata caprese

the wonderful salads (*insalata*) here, there are two famous cold dishes from the area. The *insalata caprese* is the essence of simplicity, relying on quality *mozzarella di bufala*, tomatoes and aromatic basil. *Caponata* may include marinated aubergine (eggplant), artichoke hearts and capers, with bread to soak up the flavours.

5 Pizza

Perhaps it's the water, or the quality of the flour or yeast used, but Neapolitan pizza is inimitable. It's spongy, chewy, succulent and melts in your mouth, while the toppings are flavourful and aromatic. Purists insist that it was invented here centuries ago and that the only true pizza is the *margherita* – tomato, basil and mozzarella cheese, with olive oil.

Neapolitan pizza

Spaghetti alle vongole veraci

3 Secondo

Main course dishes come in two varieties, *mare* (sea) and *terra* (land). Fresh seafood, especially *vongole* (clams) and *cozze* (mussels), are popular along the coast. Meat dishes are varied and include *polpette* (meatballs), *salsiccia* (sausage) with broccoli and *coniglio* (rabbit), a speciality on Ischia.

4 Insalata

Besides the host of fresh leaves and cherry tomatoes that end up in

6 Fish and Seafood

This category is the area's strong point. *Calamari* (squid) are a favourite, as are *cozze* (mussels) in a variety of presentations. *Seppie* (cuttle-fish) and *polipo* (octopus) are popular, too, stewed, fried or steamed. *Pesce all'acqua pazza* (fish in "crazy water") is a treat – fresh fish stewed in water with tomatoes, garlic and chillies.

7 Formaggi

Mozzarella di bufala is the signature cheese from the area. The milk of the buffalo has a tangy quality and the cheese a unique smoothness. The smoked version is *provola*.

Antipasti of olives and cured meats

8 Antipasti

The first course may be marinated fish or seafood, a selection of olives and cured meats, *bruschetta* (toasted bread) with various toppings or *prosciutto* (ham) with figs or melon, depending on the season.

9 Dolci

Many Neapolitan desserts are inspired by their Sicilian cousins, notably *delizie*, a cream-filled cake, and *pannacotta* (cooked cream), perhaps topped with fresh fruit. In season, the melon, figs and wild strawberries are unforgettable.

10 Pastries

A *sfogliatella* (pastry filled with ricotta cheese) is a sublime way to start the day, accompanied by a cup of coffee. Other treats include *babà* (cake soaked in rum and honey) and *zeppole* (pastry filled with custard and topped with wild cherries).

TOP 10 LOCAL DRINKS

1 White Wine
Campania wines are of a very high quality. Falanghina, Greco di Tufo and Lacryma Christi are reliable names.

2 Red Wine
Full-bodied reds come from the local Aglianico grape.

3 Liqueurs
The most famous of these is the lemon liqueur *limoncello*, which delivers quite a kick.

4 Beer
All major brands are available, but a local Italian favourite is Peroni. If you want draught, ask for *alla spina*.

5 Mineral Water
Italians enjoy a huge array of mineral waters. A great choice is Ferrarelle – or for something lighter, Uliveto.

6 Digestivi
Many restaurants produce their own digestive concoctions – pure alcohol with a soothing mixture of spices and flavourings.

7 Coffee
Neapolitan-style coffee traditionally comes already sweetened, and it is generally very concentrated.

8 Soft Drinks
The usual range of choices is available, but an interesting Italian cola-type drink is Chinotto.

9 Infusioni
Camomilla (camomile) is considered to be a relaxant, while other herbal teas on offer include *menta* (peppermint) and *tiglio* (lime-tree).

10 Spremute
Most bars are set up, in summer, to turn out freshly squeezed orange juice and a local version of lemonade.

Limoncello for sale

Neapolitan Souvenirs

Coral and Cameos

The tradition of miniature carvings in stone is an ancient one – the Romans (and their Renaissance imitators) used precious and semiprecious stones, from agate to emerald, as well as layered glass. Today the tradition *(see p96)* primarily focuses on gems from the sea. Coral is prized for its rich colours and soft texture, while shells are fashioned into delicate cameos.

Handmade Paper and Cards

Amalfi was once home to a thriving paper industry, which features at the Museo della Carta *(see p47)*. The tradition is still on display in local shops selling handmade paper, stationery and beautiful journals.

A traditional ceramic plate

Antiques

The area remains one of the great sources for antiques; especially plentiful are Baroque and Rococo furniture, as well as Empire pieces. Antique ceramics, too, are a good buy, notably handpainted tiles.

Shopping for antiques in Naples

Copies of Antiquities

Believe it or not, souvenir stalls outside archaeological sites – notably Pompeii – can be good sources of creditable copies of famous Roman sculptures, but you'll need to pick through the junk and be prepared to bargain.

Ceramics

Ceramics – both copies of traditional designs and original creations – are notable in Capri, Ravello and Vietri.

Gouaches

Gouache is a watercolour paint applied to heavy paper that gives a very soft yet vibrant look to the surface of a painting. In the 19th century gouache land-scapes of Naples, its bay and Vesuvius were produced in great numbers and many are still available at reasonable prices. These were the postcard souvenirs for Grand Tour visitors, and to the modern eye they evoke a sense of idyllic charm. There are also prints of the more famous scenes.

Gold

Italian artisans have been famed for centuries for their goldwork. Neapolitan artists have inherited these traditions since ancient times and local jewellery shops attest to the beauty of their creations. All gold used is at least 18 carat and prices are comparable with those in other countries, while the quality is higher. Head for Borgo degli Orefici, the Goldsmiths' District.

Figures depicting a nativity scene

8 Nativity Figures

For centuries Naples has been internationally noted for its production of figures for nativity scenes, many produced by the very best sculptors, especially in the 18th century, and reproduced to this day by skilled artisans whose *botteghe* (workshops) line the streets of the old town. A popular secular figure, done in a variety of media, including terracotta, *papier mâché*, wood, or a combination of materials, is Pulcinella *(see p44)*. There are also delightful puppets, dolls and masks.

Cobbler crafting sandals, Capri

9 Handmade Sandals, Capri

There are a number of cobblers on the island of Capri *(see p106)* who will make made-to-measure sandals within a matter of hours.

10 Intarsio, Sorrento

Renowned for centuries for its gorgeous *intarsio* (marquetry), Sorrento continues the tradition to this day, and some of the pieces are true works of art.

TOP 10 MARKETS

1 La Pignasecca, Naples
MAP M3 ▪ Via Pignasecca
▪ 8am–1pm daily
One of Naples' oldest markets and as cheap as it gets.

2 San Pasquale, Naples
MAP K6 ▪ Via S Pasquale
▪ 8am–2pm Mon, Wed, Fri–Sat
Spices, fish, clothing and jewellery.

3 Fiera Antiquaria Napoletana, Naples
MAP K6 ▪ Villa Comunale
▪ 7am–2pm 3rd Sun of month
As much junk as antiques, but great fun.

4 Atignano, Naples
MAP K2 ▪ Via Luca Giordano, Vomero ▪ 8am–2pm Mon–Sat
Household items.

5 Poggioreale
MAP L1 ▪ Via M di Caramanico
▪ 8am–2pm Mon, Fri–Sat
Piles of everything, especially shoes.

6 Posillipo
MAP K1 ▪ Viale Virgilio
▪ 8am–2pm Thu
Clothing, shoes and bags.

7 Resina, Ercolano
MAP L2 ▪ Via Pugliano
▪ 8am–1pm daily
Roman "antiques".

8 Mercato delle Pulci, Poggioreale
MAP K1 ▪ Via de Roberto
▪ 8am–1pm Sun
As much trash as treasure, but you're sure to find something.

9 Corso Giuseppe Garibaldi, Naples
MAP R1 ▪ 7am–2pm daily
A mind-boggling range of stuff.

10 Market in Amalfi
MAP E5 ▪ 8am–1pm Wed (except Aug)
Clothing and food; a truly local shopping experience.

Fresh produce at Amalfi market

Naples and the Amalfi Coast for Free

Views over Marina Grande, Sorrento, with Mount Vesuvius on the horizon

1 Marina Grande, Sorrento
MAP D5

Sorrento's Marina Grande harbour is one of the most charming spots in town, with its rows of colourful fishing boats bobbing in the water and multihued homes that were once home to fisherman.

2 Castel dell'Ovo, Naples

With a scenic setting on an islet in the Bay of Naples, entrance to the Castel dell'Ovo is free, and everyone in the family will enjoy exploring the castle while taking in the outstanding views (see p88).

3 Villa Romana, Minori

For a glimpse of ancient Roman history on the Amalfi Coast, visit the ruins of a wealthy family villa that have been excavated in the heart of Minori (see p105).

4 Spaccanapoli, Naples
MAP P2

This narrow main street cuts straight through the historic centre of the city and captures the vibrant atmosphere that is Naples. Enjoy a stroll past fine monuments while visiting free churches like the Gesù Nuovo and San Domenico Maggiore (see p80). Today the street is officially named Via Benedetto Croce and moving east it changes to Via S Biagio dei Librai (see pp76–85).

5 Via Positanesi d'America, Positano
MAP E5

Connecting Positano's Spiaggia Grande with the more secluded Spiaggia di Fornillo (see p62), this cliff-hugging pathway is one of the prettiest walks on the Amalfi Coast.

6 Galleria Umberto I, Naples

The soaring glass roof, Neo-Renaissance designs and marble floors of the Galleria Umberto I make this 19th-century shopping gallery worth seeing for its architecture alone (see p88).

Galleria Umberto I, Naples

7 Auditorium Oscar Niemeyer, Ravello

MAP E4 ■ Via della Repubblica 12
■ 089 85 83 60

This rare example of modern design is named after its creator, Brazilian architect Oscar Niemeyer. While only open for events, its large terrace offers the same outstanding views you would pay to see at the Villa Rufolo nearby.

8 Arco Naturale, Capri

MAP C5

While the price tag of many of Capri's sights can shock, the natural beauty is as easy on the eyes as it is on the budget. For a beautiful walk, follow signs from the Piazzetta in Capri Town to the Arco Naturale *(see p34)*.

Arco Naturale, Capri

9 Duomo, Naples

While there is an admission charge to visit the cathedral's museum and archaeological area, it is free to visit the soaring nave of the Duomo and the dazzling Cappella di San Gennaro *(see pp16–17)*.

10 Villa Comunale, Naples

This 18th-century urban park was designed by Luigi Vanvitelli, the mastermind behind the grandiose Reggia di Caserta. With playgrounds, classic statues and beautiful views, it's a family friendly spot to while away an afternoon *(see p88)*.

TOP 10 MONEY-SAVING TIPS

Street food, Naples

1 Naples is famous for its street food, which is a delicious way to save money and experience local specialities.

2 Visit Naples from October to April (but not Christmas) when low-season rates and discounts will delight the budget-minded traveller.

3 Note that many hotels and restaurants on the Amalfi Coast and Capri close during the winter, however, rates are often lower for the shoulder season October to November and February to March.

4 Most beaches have a *spiaggia libera* area where you do not have to pay to access the beach.

5 Parking can be exceedingly expensive and limited on the Amalfi Coast, so traveling by public transport is recommended.

6 Save money on visits to many sights in Naples and throughout the region with the Campania Artecard, see www.campaniartecard.it.

7 Take the Circumvesuviana train for an inexpensive way to travel between Naples, Sorrento, Pompeii and Herculaneum.

8 The ferry between Positano and Amalfi is an affordable way to see the beauty of the Amalfi Coast from the sea.

9 Alibus runs a cheap shuttle from the Naples airport to the Napoli Centrale train station and port.

10 Many museums and archaeological sites offer a free open day during the week or month.

🔟 Religious Celebrations

La Befana, festival of the Epiphany

1 La Befana
6 Jan

In Italy the festival of the Epiphany is personified by La Befana, a witch-like hag flying in on a broom who delivers gifts to good children and puts "lumps of coal" (actually sweets) in the shoes of naughty ones.

2 Carnevale
Feb

Pulcinella *(see p44)* is lord of this blow-out in Naples, just before the austerities of Lent begin. Lasagne is the dish to indulge in, and masks and partying are very much a part of this age-old celebration. Kids get the chance to choose their fantasy persona and parade around in their finery.

Pucinella figurines, Carnevale

3 Pasqua
Mar or Apr

In Italy, Pasqua (Easter Sunday) and Pasquetta (Easter Monday) are both important, as is the week leading up to them in some towns. Good Friday processions are held around the Naples area, with an especially rich one on the island of Procida. Pasquetta is traditionally a day for outings – picnics being a top choice to celebrate the advent of spring. Near Sant'Anastasia, 15 km (9 miles) east of Naples, a festival is held at the sanctuary of the Madonna dell'Arco.

4 San Gennaro

The Saturday before the first Sunday in May is the first of a thrice-yearly event. During this celebration, the blood of Naples' patron saint – who has seen the city through earthquakes, volcanic eruptions and football championships – flows again. The miracle is received with a hysteria seldom seen in this day and age – a manifestation of age-old faith that involves flower-bedecked processions of the saint's effigy through the old quarter.

5 San Giovanni
24 Jun

The feast day of St John the Baptist also sometimes sees his blood boil – a phial of it is ensconced in the church of San Gregorio Armeno *(see p80)*. Otherwise, the saint is traditionally remembered in charmingly pagan ways, linked to the summer solstice: night bathing, magicians and the gathering of walnuts to make *nocino*, a liqueur prepared for late autumn.

6 Santa Maria del Carmine
15–17 Jul

Every summer, Naples' tallest bell tower is "burned" in commemoration of a legend that recounts how an icon kept here, the Madonna Bruna, saved it from being destroyed by fire. An array of fireworks are dramatically set off at the climax of the festivities *(see p80)*.

7 Ferragosto
15 Aug

The Assumption of the Virgin Mary marks the height of the summer season, when most shops and restaurants close in the city (although not on the coast). Pozzuoli stages a contest of climbing a greased pole, while Positano re-enacts a landing of Saracen corsairs.

8 Madonna di Piedigrotta
Sep

Once a fancy affair, today the event involves a song competition and theatrical events, plus fireworks and street parties. It all centres on a 14th-century sculpture of the Madonna and Child.

9 L'Immacolata
8 Dec

Celebrating the Immaculate Conception, this festival opens the Christmas season; nativity scenes and decorations go up and the Guglia dell' Immacolata (see p78) in Piazza del Gesù becomes the focal point of activity.

Guglia dell'Immacolata

10 Natale
24–25 Dec

At Christmas the streets around San Gregorio Armeno (see p80) are full of shoppers looking for items to complete their nativity scenes, and concerts take place in the churches.

Christmas nativity scene

TOP 10 SECULAR FESTIVALS

Festival delle Ville Vesuviane

1 Regata Storica, Amalfi
Jun
Every four years Amalfi hosts a boat race against Venice, Pisa and Genoa.

2 Culture Week
Apr
For one week publicly owned museums, historic and archaeological sites are free.

3 Maggio dei Monumenti
May
Churches and buildings usually closed to the public open for one week.

4 Estate a Napoli
Summer in Naples includes outdoor films, theatre and music.

5 Concerti al Tramonto, Villa San Michele, Anacapri
May–Aug
This genteel villa is the venue for sunset classical concerts (see p35).

6 Music Festival of Villa Rufolo, Ravello
Jun–Sep
A rich calendar of music, theatre and dance in evocative settings (see p37).

7 Neapolis Festival
Jul
Southern Italy's largest rockfest invades the area of Bagnoli.

8 Festival delle Ville Vesuviane
Jul
The aristocratic villas along this coast play host to classical concerts (see p96).

9 Pizzafest, Naples
Sep
A celebration of the city's famous dish, as pizza-makers spin their dough.

10 Capodanno, Naples
31 Dec
New Year's Eve involves merrymaking and fireworks over Castel dell'Ovo.

Naples and the Amalfi Coast Area by Area

Procida, crammed with ancient
buildings painted in lively colours

TOP 10 Spaccanapoli to Capodimonte

The ancient heart of the city is celebrated for its striking juxtaposition of chaos and consummate artistry, but most of all for the sheer, boundless energy of the Neapolitan spirit. In many ways, it is an atavistic realm, ruled by its past, including innumerable disasters, but it is also a city with an awareness of its abiding glories, and Old Naples has opened anew to the world. Its narrow streets are much safer and cleaner than before and its erstwhile dilapidated, shut-away treasures are now restored and far better organized, without losing any of their uniquely vibrant feeling. Spaccanapoli is the colloquial name for the long, narrow street that runs from Via Duomo to Via Monteoliveto and is the remnant of an ancient Greco-Roman thoroughfare.

Statue, Museo Archeologico

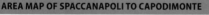

AREA MAP OF SPACCANAPOLI TO CAPODIMONTE

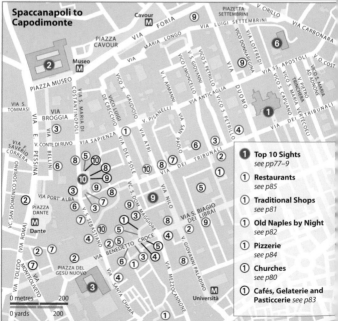

1 **Top 10 Sights**
see pp77–9

1 **Restaurants**
see p85

1 **Traditional Shops**
see p81

1 **Old Naples by Night**
see p82

1 **Pizzerie**
see p84

1 **Churches**
see p80

1 **Cafés, Gelaterie and Pasticcerie** see p83

0 metres 200
0 yards 200

Impressive interior of the Duomo

1 Duomo

Although its position in the present-day street-plan seems to be an afterthought and the perfunctory Neo-Gothic façade is less than inspiring, inside Naples' cathedral is a fascinating cornucopia of history, art and culture. There are ancient remains of the Greek and Roman cities to explore, including some beautiful paleo-Christian mosaics in the baptistry, and splendid art abounds in the main church and its chapels, including the huge work dedicated to the city's patron saint, Gennaro (Januarius) (see pp16–17).

2 Museo Archeologico

One of the world's most important museums of ancient art houses some of the most famous statues from the Greco-Roman past, such as the Callipygean Venus that set standards of physical beauty that have endured through the ages. Other monumental marble works include the Farnese Hercules, but the collections also feature bronzes, mosaics, frescoes, carved semiprecious stone, glassware, Greek vases and Egyptian artifacts (see pp18–21).

Cloister tiles detail, Santa Chiara

3 Santa Chiara

MAP N3 ▪ Via Santa Chiara 49c ▪ 081 551 66 73 ▪ Open 7:30am–1pm, 4:30–8pm daily (church); 9:30am–7:30pm Mon–Sat, 10am–2:30pm Sun & public hols (museum & cloister) ▪ Adm (church free) ▪ DA ▪ www.monasterodisantachiara.com

The façade of this structure, rebuilt after World War II, is like a huge cliff of buff-coloured tufa, relieved only by its portico and giant rose window. Only the base of its 14th-century bell tower is original. Inside the decor has been returned to its Gothic origins, since all the Baroque embellishment was destroyed in wartime bombings. The tomb of Robert of Anjou is the largest funerary monument of medieval Italy, and behind this is the delightful tiled cloister (see p50).

North Naples

Real Bosco di Capodimonte

A56

Capodimonte

④ CAPODIMONTE

Orto Botanico ⑧

VERGINI

Palazzo dello Spagnolo

AVVOCATA ⑤

⑦

Area of Spaccanapoli to Capodimonte map

Ⓜ Museo   ④ Garibaldi Ⓜ

⑩ Napoli Centrale Ⓜ

① ⑦

Ⓜ Dante   Porta Nolana Ⓜ

⑩

⑥ Ⓜ Università   ⑩

⑥

⑩ Gulf of Naples

Ⓜ Toledo

Ⓜ Municipio

Augusteo

SAN FERDINANDO

0 metres   800
0 yards   800

4 Capodimonte

This impressive royal palace is home to important works by some of the greatest masters, including Botticelli, Filippino Lippi, Mantegna, Bellini, Fra' Bartolomeo, Michelangelo, Raphael, Titian, Rembrandt and Dürer, as well as by every great painter working in Naples during the 17th and 18th centuries, including Caravaggio and Vivarini *(see pp22–3).*

Virgin with Child Enthroned **(1465) by Bartolomeo Vivarini, Capodimonte**

5 Palazzo dello Spagnolo

MAP P1 ▪ Via Vergini 19

Dating from 1728, this palace offers a fine example of a well-known Neapolitan architectural element, the so-called staircase *"ad ali di falco"* (with falcon wings). Separating two courtyards, the external stairway consists of double flights of steps with tiers of archways, a theatrical feature that became the trademark of its designer, Ferdinando Sanfelice. Stucco designs can be seen throughout; particular attention to detail is evident above doorways.

6 Santi Apostoli

MAP P1 ▪ Largo Santi Apostoli 9 ▪ Open 8:30am–1pm, 4:30–8pm Mon–Sat; 9am–1pm Sun

The original church on this site is believed to have been built in the 5th century over a Roman temple to Mercury. It was rebuilt in the 17th century, with decoration added over the next 100 years. As such it provides a complete treasury of

---

THE THREE GUGLIE

The area's three *guglie* ("needles" or "spires") imitate the original towering contraptions built in the 1600s and 1700s to celebrate feast days. The first stone *guglia* was raised to San Gennaro, when the saint supposedly saved Naples from Vesuvius's fury in 1631. Next came one dedicated to San Domenico, as thanks for the end of the 1656 plague. The last adorns Piazza del Gesù, dedicated to the Immaculate Virgin.

17th- and 18th-century art, not just by Neapolitan artists but by some of the greatest masters of the day. Most famous is the fresco cycle by Lanfranco, with a marvellous trompe-l'oeil architectural setting by Codazzi. Another highlight is the altar that was designed by Borromini.

7 San Giovanni a Carbonara

MAP Q1 ▪ Via Carbonara 5 ▪ Open 9:30am–1pm Mon–Sat

This 14th-century church has no façade of its own but is reached by a double staircase through a courtyard to the left of the Chapel of Santa Monica. Inside are a circular chapel with 15th-century frescoes and bas-reliefs by Spanish masters Bartolomé Ordoñez and Diego de Siloe.

Chapel, San Giovanni a Carbonara

8 Orto Botanico

MAP K1 ■ Via Floria 223 ■ 081 253 39 37 ■ Open 9am–2pm Mon–Fri by appt only ■ Guided tours Mar–May ■ www.ortobotanico.unina.it

Created in 1807, this botanical garden is one of Italy's most important, both in size and in its collections. Given Naples' climate, it has been possible to cultivate examples of nearly all of the world's plants and flowers here. Historic structures include the Neo-Classical Serra Temperata, built in 1807 and the double stairway entrance to the grounds.

Cactus display, Orto Botanico

9 Sansevero Chapel

MAP P2 ■ Via Francesco de Sanctis 19 ■ 081 552 49 36 ■ Open 10am–5:40pm Mon, Wed–Sat; 10am–1:10pm Sun ■ Adm ■ www.museosansevero.it

Few spaces are decorated with such unity as this family chapel, designed by the eccentric 18th-century prince Raimondo di Sangro. Full of allegorical symbolism, the statuary are among Naples' most famous, particularly the "veiled" figures of Christ and Modesty. Don't miss the Anatomical Machines.

10 Piazza Bellini

MAP N2

One of the most appealing places in Naples is lined with cafés, bookshops and palaces. Of particular note is the monastery of Sant'Antonio a Port'Alba, incorporating 15th-century Palazzo Conca. At the centre of the piazza, in addition to a statue of the eponymous composer, is an archaeological excavation, revealing 5th-century BC Greek walls of large tufa blocks (see p52).

A MORNING AT OLD NAPLES' CHURCHES

▶ Begin your tour of Naples' two oldest main streets at **Piazza del Gesù Nuovo**, where you can admire the Guglia dell'Immacolata and the rusticated façade of the **Gesù Nuovo** (see p80). Further along, enter **Santa Chiara** (see p77) to take in the medieval tombs and then around the back to see the famous tiled cloister.

Continuing on, stop for a drink at one of the cafés in **Piazza San Domenico**, where you will note that the Guglia di San Domenico has mermaids sculpted on its base. Across the street, stop in at the church of **Sant'Angelo a Nilo** (see p80) to see its Donatello bas-relief, and at the next corner, look for the ancient statue of the god of the Nile, known familiarly as "The Body of Naples". Follow the street all the way to **Via Duomo**, pausing at the shops of all kinds along the way.

Next, visit the culturally amazing **Duomo** (see pp16–17), and then go behind it to see the earliest *guglia*, topped by a statue of San Gennaro, and Caravaggio's revolutionary painting *The Acts of Mercy* in the **Pio Monte della Misericordia** (see p51). Double back along **Via dei Tribunali**, where you can visit more fascinating churches, including **San Gregorio Armeno** (see p80) and **Santa Maria delle Anime del Purgatorio ad Arco** (see p80).

Finally, head for **Piazza Bellini**, where you can watch the world go by and have a drink or a full meal at one of the friendly cafés.

See map on pp76–7

Churches

Detail of the elaborate ceiling, San Lorenzo Maggiore

1 San Lorenzo Maggiore
MAP P2 ▪ Via dei Tribunali 316
▪ Open 9:30am–5:30pm daily

One of Naples' oldest monuments, the church is a mix of Gothic and Baroque styles. In the cloister there is access to Greco-Roman remains.

2 Gesù Nuovo
MAP N3 ▪ Piazza del Gesù 2 ▪ Open 7:15am–1pm, 4:15–7:15pm daily

The wall of this church dates back to a 15th-century fortified palace. Inside are works of art from the 16th to 19th centuries.

3 San Domenico Maggiore
MAP N2 ▪ Vico S Domenico Maggiore 18 ▪ Open 9:30am–noon Tue–Thu & Sun; also 4:30–5pm Fri & Sat

Highlights at this 13th-century church include frescoes by Pietro Cavallini.

4 Sant'Angelo a Nilo
MAP P2 ▪ Piazzetta Nilo
▪ Open 9:30am–noon daily

This 14th-century church houses the *Assumption of the Virgin* by Donatello.

5 San Gregorio Armeno
MAP P2 ▪ Via S Gregorio Armeno 1 ▪ Open 9am–noon Mon–Fri; 9am–12:30pm Sat–Sun

This church is best known for the cult of St Patricia, whose blood "liquefies" each Tuesday. It also has a beautiful cloister.

6 San Paolo Maggiore
MAP P2 ▪ Piazza S Gaetano 76
▪ Open 8am–noon, 5–7pm daily

The 8th-century church still retains two Corinthian columns and features an annexed sanctuary.

7 Santa Maria delle Anime del Purgatorio ad Arco
MAP P2 ▪ Via dei Tribunali 39
▪ Open 9:30am–1pm Mon–Fri, 10am–5pm Sat ▪ Adm

The railings outside are adorned with bronze skulls, evoking the tradition of care for the dead.

8 San Pietro a Maiella
MAP N2 ▪ Piazza Luigi Miraglia 393 ▪ Open 7:30am–noon, 5:30–7pm Mon–Sat, 8:30am–1pm Sun

Built in the 1300s, San Pietro underwent a Baroque makeover in the 1600s and then was returned to Gothic style in the 1900s.

9 Santa Maria di Donnaregina Vecchia
MAP P1 ▪ Vico Donnaregina 26
▪ Open 10am–7pm Wed–Fri, 10am–noon Sat & Sun

This fine 13th-century church contains some Cavallini frescoes.

10 Santa Maria del Carmine
MAP R3 ▪ Piazza del Carmine 2
▪ Open 6:30am–12:30pm, 4–7:30pm daily; summer: until 8:30pm daily

Home to the Madonna Bruna icon, the focus of a Naples cult.

Traditional Shops

1 A.S.
MAP N3 ■ Vico Pallonetto a Santa Chiara 38

You never know what you'll find in the way of old prints and period objects here – or if you'll find the shop as it doesn't have a sign outside! You might uncover an 18th-century engraving or a 1930s Art Deco-style poster.

2 Napul'é
MAP P2 ■ Via dei Tribunali 90

Take the opportunity to see crafts-men at work at this little *bottega* (workshop), refining the lifelike details of wonderful nativity figures. Most of them are replicas of famous originals, but they will also create personalized versions to order.

3 Melinoi
MAP N3 ■ Via B Croce 34

An upmarket outlet for stylish clothing, which includes a comprehensive range of designer labels from Italy, France and Spain.

4 Osmis
MAP N3 ■ Via Santa Chiara 10F

This little shop carries a charming line of locally and internationally crafted jewellery, masks, lamps, mirrors and candles.

5 Affaitati
MAP N3 ■ Via B Croce 21 & Via Costantinopoli 18

One of Old Naples' finest antiques shops. Specialities are furniture and ceramics from the 16th to the 19th centuries. Nativity figures are also on offer.

Ceramic piece, Affaitati

6 Decumano
MAP N3
■ Via Croce Benedetto 30

This large store specializes in reproductions of Capodimonte porcelain, as well as other ceramic art from Naples' illustrious past.

7 Via San Sebastiano Shops
MAP N2

Along this street, just off Piazza Bellini, you'll find Neapolitan musical instruments, from mandolins to the *triccaballacco* (a three-pronged clacker with cymbals attached).

Guitars for sale, Via San Sebastiano

8 Tattoo Records
MAP P2 ■ Piazzetta Nilo 15

In an appealing little piazza just off Spaccanapoli, this funky music shop is good if you're looking for CDs of local music or rare imports. The proprietor will help you find everything from traditional *tarantella* music to the latest Neapolitan rockers.

9 Nel Regno di Pulcinella
MAP N2 ■ Vico S Domenico Maggiore 9

This little shop is crammed full of *Pulcinella* figures (see p46) in all shapes and sizes, from the sweetly innocent to the bawdy. All in keeping with the character's personality.

10 Scriptura
MAP N2
■ Via San Sebastiano 22

This small shop sells handmade leather products, including high-quality bags, wallets and diaries. The beautifully packaged items make great gifts to take home.

See map on pp76–7

Old Naples by Night

1 Kestè
MAP P3 = Largo S
Giovanni Maggiore 26–7
This lively bar with a friendly atmosphere is open all day long for cocktails and beers. It attracts a student crowd, who dance to live bands and spill out onto the square in summer.

Vibrant decor at Velvet Zone

2 Kinky Klub
MAP N3 = Vicolo
della Quercia 26
A larger incarnation of Naples' historic Kinky Bar, this reggae club is not at all kinky as its name suggests. Head to the lower level to enjoy the Caribbean sounds, dancing and live music.

3 La Tana dell' Arte
MAP N2 = Via Bellini 30
Opposite Naples' fine arts academy, the name of this restaurant and cocktail bar means "The Den of Art". The charming setting and outdoor terrace attract an artistic crowd.

4 Galleria 19
MAP N2 = Via San Sebastiano
19 = Closed Mon & in summer
This subterranean club draws a young crowd who come for the DJ-spun mix of house music, electronic sounds and art film screenings.

5 Evaluna Libreria Cafè
MAP N2 = Piazza Bellini 72
A favourite in the historical centre, this bar-cum-café offers fun and culture to its clientele, who come here to read books and magazines while sipping coffees or cocktails.

6 Bourbon Street
MAP N2 = Via Bellini 52
= Closed Mon & Jul–Aug
This large jazz club features local talent every evening. In summer Bourbon Street organizes jazz cruises around the bay.

7 Velvet Zone
MAP N3 = Via Cisterna dell'Olio
11 = Closed Mon & Jun–mid-Sep
The "Velvet" is the top club in the old quarter for dancing, since it stays open until 6am at weekends. Music varies from techno to 1980s to rock, and to live music from time to time.

8 Spazio Nea
MAP N2 = Via Costantinopoli 53
Located just steps from Piazza Bellini, a lively area after dark, this contemporary gallery is a gathering spot for artistic types. Overflowing with atmosphere, there's indoor and outdoor seating areas, a café and Wi-Fi. They also host theatre, peformances and special events.

9 Perditempo
MAP N2 = Via San Pietro a
Maiella 8 = Closed Sun
This intimate bar-bookshop-music store is anything but a "waste of time" as its name might suggest. An eclectic music soundtrack accompanies the stimulating conversation and good drinks.

10 Mamamù
MAP P3 = Via Sedile Di Porto 46
A live music hot spot for the young music scene, which showcases indie rock, punk and electric music. Mamamù organizes a popular summer rock festival every June.

Cafés, Gelaterie and Pasticcerie

 Gran Caffè Aragonese
MAP N2 ■ Piazza S Domenico Maggiore 5–8

This café dominates the scene on a beautiful and crowded piazza. It offers a good range of local desserts and savoury snacks, and excellent Neapolitan-style coffee.

 Bar Mexico
MAP N2 ■ Piazza Dante 86

Bar Mexico is a local favourite reputed to have the best espresso in town, but if you don't want it sweetened *(alla napoletana)* then ask for a *caffè amaro* (bitter coffee). A hot-weather winner is the *frappe di caffè* (iced whipped coffee). You can also stock up on some wonderful coffee blends to take home.

③ Caffè dell'Epoca
MAP N2 ■ Via Sta Maria di Costantinopoli 82

Dating back to 1886, this place knows all about quality. Enjoy an *espresso* and a *cornetto* (croissant) at one of the outside tables – or make like a local and stand at the bar.

④ Gay-Odin
MAP N3 ■ Via B Croce 61

A Naples institution that is a paradise for chocolate lovers. Try the hot chocolate or the divine ice cream.

Gay-Odin chocolate shop

⑤ Scaturchio
MAP N2 ■ Piazza S Domenico Maggiore 19

Noted all over Naples for its wonderful traditional pastries, it's a real treat to sample the wares while checking out this piazza. Don't arrive too late or they might have sold out.

Scrumptious pastries at Scaturchio

 Gelateria della Scimmia
MAP N3 ■ Piazza Carità 4

This is one of the city's oldest and most famous *gelaterie* (ice-cream parlours) so expect a crowd.

⑦ Xeo Cafe
MAP N3 ■ Piazza Sette Settembre 20/21

A unique blend of bar and *gelaterie*, here you'll find freshly made, all natural gelato served as ice lollies, which is quite the novelty in Italy.

⑧ Intra Moenia
MAP N2 ■ Piazza Bellini 70

A good place to hang out and enjoy a drink. In warm weather it's also a lively gay venue in the evenings.

⑨ Caffè Arabo
MAP N2 ■ Piazza Bellini 64

Not just a great café with an appealing atmosphere, but a purveyor of tasty Arabic goodies and full meals.

⑩ Internetbar
MAP N2 ■ Piazza Bellini 74

This trendy establishment offers Internet facilities, drinks and snacks, as well as an art gallery.

See map on pp76–7 ←

Pizzerie

1 L'Antica Pizzeria "da Michele"

MAP Q2 ■ Via Cesare Sersale 1–3 ■ 081 553 92 04 ■ Closed Sun ■ No credit cards ■ €

The most traditional of Naples' *pizzerie*. The menu is limited to only two varieties, *margherita* and *marinara*. Still, the taste is sublime – and the wait often considerable. Take a number at the door before queuing. Tables are shared.

2 Lombardi a Santa Chiara

MAP N3 ■ Via B Croce 59 ■ 081 552 07 80 ■ Closed Tue ■ €

Follow the locals downstairs to eat fresh pizza either standing up or sat on stools. Avoid the pricey restaurant.

3 Di Matteo

MAP P2 ■ Via dei Tribunali 94 ■ 081 45 52 62 ■ No credit cards ■ €

As well as pizza, try some *frittura* here – deep-fried tidbits of vegetables, rice and cheese.

4 Pizzeria del Presidente

MAP P2 ■ Via dei Tribunali 120–1 ■ 081 21 09 03 ■ Closed Sun ■ No credit cards ■ €

Another *pizzeria* on this busy street, which gained its moment of fame when then US President Bill Clinton stopped by for a snack.

5 Pizzeria Starita

MAP M1 ■ Via Materdei 27–28 ■ 081 557 36 82 ■ Closed Sun L ■ €

One of the oldest *pizzerie* in Naples, this place is famous for its *antipasti* and fresh pizzas. The *angioletti fritti* (fried angels) is a popular item, too. Expect a queue, especially weekends.

6 Antica Pizzeria Port'Alba

MAP N2 ■ Via Port'Alba 18 ■ 081 45 97 13 ■ €

Through an archway off Piazza Dante, this *pizzerie* even has a traditional wood-fired oven with lava stones from Mount Vesuvius.

7 Pizzeria Trianon da Ciro

MAP Q2 ■ Via Pietro Colletta 42–6 ■ 081 553 94 26 ■ No credit cards ■ €

Every bit as traditional as "da Michele" – and just across the street – this eatery is more upmarket, with a larger choice. The decor recalls the city's *belle époque* heyday.

Pizzeria Trianon da Ciro

8 Pizzeria Sorbillo

MAP N2 ■ Via dei Tribunali 32 ■ 081 44 66 43 ■ Closed Sun ■ No credit cards ■ €

The main restaurant is modern but the stand-up branch next door dates from 1935. Here you can be entertained by pizza makers who twirl the dough, dash on the topping and pop it into the brick oven.

9 Pizzeria Vesi

MAP P2 ■ Via S. Biagio dei Librai 115 ■ 081 551 10 35 ■ No credit cards ■ €

Pizzeria Vesi specializes in "pizza DOC" – a delicious aromatic union of mozzarella balls, *pomodorini* (cherry tomatoes) and basil.

10 Pizzeria Fortuna

MAP R2 ■ Via PS Mancini 8 ■ 081 20 53 80 ■ Closed Sun ■ No credit cards ■ €

Little more than a counter with a few plastic tables in front, this little place turns out delicious *pizzette* and other goodies in seconds.

Restaurants

(1) Cantina della Sapienza
MAP N2 ▪ Via della Sapienza 40 ▪ 081 45 90 78 ▪ Closed D, Sun, Aug ▪ No credit cards ▪ €

The menu changes daily here but is always authentic. Dishes such as *melanzane alla parmigiana* (aubergine/eggplant with mozzarella and tomato) make a regular appearance.

(2) La Cantina del Sole
MAP P3 ▪ Via G Paladino 3 ▪ 081 552 73 12 ▪ Closed Mon, Tue–Sat L, Aug ▪ €€

A favourite with the locals, this restaurant is noted for recipes that date back to the 1600s.

(3) Bellini
MAP N2 ▪ Via Santa Maria di Costantinopoli 79–80 ▪ 081 45 97 74 ▪ Closed Sun, 1 wk Aug ▪ €€

This *trattoria* specializes in seafood pasta and grilled catch of the day. Pizza also available.

(4) Mimì alla Ferrovia
MAP R1 ▪ Via Alfonso d'Aragona 19 ▪ 081 553 85 25 ▪ Closed Aug, 2 wks Aug ▪ €€

Mimì specializes in fish and seafood, but they also have great *pasta e ceci* (soup with chickpeas).

Seafood dish at Mimì alla Ferrovia

PRICE CATEGORIES
For a three-course meal for one with half a bottle of wine (or equivalent meal), taxes and extra charges.
....
€ under €30   €€ €30–€50   €€€ over €50

(5) Palazzo Petrucci
MAP N2 ▪ Piazza San Domenico Maggiore 4 ▪ 081 551 24 60 ▪ €€€

Neapolitan fare with a creative touch at this Michelin-starred restaurant and adjacent *pizzerie*. Mimimalist decor complements the setting in the stables of Palazzo Petrucci.

(6) La Vecchia Cantina
MAP M3 ▪ Vico S Nicola alla Carità 13–14 ▪ 081 552 02 26 ▪ Closed Sun ▪ €

Taking full advantage of its location next to the market, this place serves seriously fresh fish at great prices.

(7) Un Sorriso Integrale
MAP N2 ▪ Vico S Pietro a Maiella 6 ▪ €€

This vegetarian café serves fresh, healthy meals, including an excellent selection of sharing plates.

(8) Neapolis
MAP P3 ▪ Via Giovanni Paladino 16 ▪ 081 551 55 84 ▪ No credit cards ▪ €

Cheap and tasty Greek dishes include kebabs and filled pitta breads, which you can eat in or take away.

(9) Lombardi
MAP P1 ▪ Via Foria 12 ▪ 081 45 62 20 ▪ Closed Mon ▪ €€

A restaurant and a *pizzerie* a bit off the beaten track, so rarely crowded. The *antipasto* buffet is wonderful, featuring seasonal delicacies.

(10) La Locanda del Grifo
MAP N2 ▪ Via Francesco del Giudice 12 ▪ 081 557 14 92 ▪ €€

Part of the Hotel Neapolis, this small *trattoria* serves Neapolitan fare using seasonal produce. The pretty patio overlooks a medieval campanile.

See map on pp76–7 ←

🔟 Toledo to Chiaia

The first impression of the area known as "Royal Naples" is of spaciousness and light. This is Naples' showcase: a vision of how functional the city can be with due appreciation for its setting. Elegant architecture from various ages graces the terrain here, which is also home to one of the most authentic neighbourhoods, maritime Santa Lucia. Above it all, the Vomero district boasts a fine castle and monastery overlooking the bay and one of the city's best parks, while to the west is the lively Mergellina district, with its working port and busy restaurants lined up along the coast.

Detail on the Triumphal Arch, Castel Nuovo

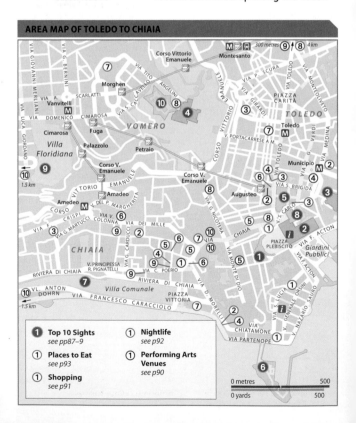

AREA MAP OF TOLEDO TO CHIAIA

1 Top 10 Sights
see pp87–9

1 Places to Eat
see p93

1 Shopping
see p91

1 Nightlife
see p92

1 Performing Arts Venues
see p90

San Francesco di Paola

exudes the delicacy of the early Renaissance. Inside, the spartan blankness is relieved by the wondrously complex ceiling of the Barons' Hall, while the fresco fragments and sculptures in the chapel juxtapose with the harsh reality of the dungeons. In addition there are fine collections of religious and secular artwork. Go up to the battlements to see the panorama *(see pp14–15)*.

① San Francesco di Paola
MAP M6 ■ Piazza del Plebiscito
■ Open 8:30am–12:30pm, 3:30–7pm
Mon–Sat

The impetus to build this imitation Pantheon came from the Napoleonic king Joachim Murat (1808–15). Completed under the reinstated Bourbon dynasty, the idea was to do away with the chaotic jumble around the palace by recreating a version of the ancient Roman temple to the gods and setting it off with arcades echoing those of St Peter's. It dominates a semicircular piazza with the Palazzo Reale at the opposite end *(see p50)*.

② Palazzo Reale
The Royal Palace is largely 18th-century in character, with its vast layout, imposing façade and important rooms such as the ballroom and the chapel. However, later embellishments took a Neo-Classical turn, in particular the marvellous grand staircase. Under Napoleonic rule many of the rooms received a thorough makeover, which dominates the decor today. Don't miss the fine Renaissance and Baroque paintings from the royal collection, including works by Guercino, Spadarino and several Flemish masters *(see pp12–13)*.

③ Castel Nuovo
This rather sombre fortress is a study in stylistic contrasts – in direct opposition to its bulky grey towers, the marble Triumphal Arch

④ Certosa di San Martino
If there is one place that could be called the true museum of Naples, this former monastery is it. So varied are the collections and the architecture that all aspects of the city's history and cultural output seem to be represented here. These include a large collection of Nativity scenes and figures, some of Naples' most significant paintings and sculptures, views of the city painted in different eras, a decorative arts collection, and the exuberantly Baroque church, decorated by the best Neapolitan artists of the 17th and 18th centuries *(see pp26–9)*.

**Stunning ceiling frescoes,
Certosa di San Martino**

Galleria Umberto I

5 Galleria Umberto I
MAP N5 ■ Piazza Trieste e Trento to Via Toledo

Part of the Urban Renewal Plan following the cholera epidemic of 1884, this light-filled space is home to elegant buildings with Neo-Renaissance embellishments and marble floors, overarched by a roof of iron and glass. Located across from the Royal Palace and Teatro San Carlo, the spot immediately became popular with the city's smart and artistic set, and even today has an air of bygone charm.

6 Castel dell'Ovo
MAP K2 ■ Via Partenope ■ Open 9am–7pm Mon–Sat, 9am–2pm Sun

In ancient times, this spot was part of the vast estate of the Roman general

---

THE BIRTH OF GRAND OPERA

Along with its many other musical accomplishments, Italy is the home of opera. Inspired by Classical Greek drama, the first opera was composed by northerner Monteverdi towards the end of the 16th century. But it was Naples, renowned for its inimitable *castrati (see p47)*, who made the genre its own. The accompanying sets, costumes and dance were refined, and the whole artform soon went international.

Lucullus. At the end of the 5th century an order of monks founded a monastery here, then the Normans built the first castle. It was modified by succeeding dynasties, achieving its present form in the 16th century. Legend has it that its name derives from a magic egg *(uovo)* hidden inside, supposedly placed there by the Roman poet Virgil. The building is now used for cultural events.

7 Villa Comunale
MAP K6 ■ Via Caracciolo ■ Open May–Oct: 7am–midnight daily; Nov–Apr: 7am–10pm daily

Designed by Luigi Vanvitelli and inaugurated in 1781 as the royal gardens, this large public park is on the bay. Graced with 19th-century copies of Classical statuary, it was once home to the monumental ancient Farnese Bull group, now in the Museo Archeologico *(see p20)*. Other adornments include a Neo-Classical aquarium; an iron and glass bandstand; and a zoological station with a turtle rescue centre.

Castel dell'Ovo

8 Teatro San Carlo

MAP N5 ■ Via San Carlo 98F
■ 081 797 21 11 ■ Open for guided tours 9am–5:30pm Thu–Mon ■ Adm

Actually an appendage to the Palazzo Reale, built by order of King Charles, this opera house predates the La Scala in Milan by some 40 years. Officially opened on 4 November 1737, it is one of the most important opera houses in the world. The interior was originally in the Bourbon colours (silver, gold and sky blue), but after being rebuilt following a fire in 1816 the colour scheme is now mostly gold and red, though no less sumptuous. The theatre contains a museum charting its history.

Auditorium, Teatro San Carlo

9 Museo Nazionale della Ceramica Duca di Martina

MAP J4 ■ Villa Floridiana, Via Cimarosa 77 ■ Open 8:30am–2:30pm Wed–Mon ■ Adm

Since 1927 this villa has been home to a prestigious collection of European and Oriental decorative art donated by the Duke of Martina. Of the 6,000 items, highlights are Hispano-Moorish lustreware, Italian majolica tiles, Limoges porcelain and 18th-century Oriental porcelain (see p49).

10 Castel Sant'Elmo

MAP L4 ■ Via Tito Angelini 22
■ Open 9am–2pm Wed–Mon ■ Adm

This Angevin castle dating from 1329 was upgraded to its six-point configuration in the 16th century, giving it a militaristic presence looming above the city. It now houses libraries, cultural activities and exhibitions.

A DAY IN ROYAL NAPLES

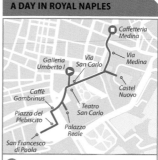

▶ MORNING

Begin your tour inside **Galleria Umberto I**, where you can enjoy a morning cappuccino at Caffè Roma (No. 25–6) and get a sense of the bustling optimism of 19th-century Naples. Coming out onto **Via San Carlo**, the elegant Neo-Classical façade of the **Teatro San Carlo** is directly across the street.

Go to the right and around the corner into **Piazza del Plebiscito**. On your right is the massive dome of the church of **San Francesco di Paola** (see p87), and on your left, **Palazzo Reale** (see pp12–13). First walk over to the church, noting the bronze equestrian statues of kings Charles III and Ferdinand I, then go back across the piazza to the Royal Palace. Enter the courtyard and take the magnificent staircase up to the apartments.

Take a break for a snack or lunch at historic **Caffè Gambrinus** (see p93), just outside the piazza.

AFTERNOON

After lunch go back past the Teatro San Carlo and the palace gardens, and be sure not to miss the giant statues of the horse-tamers at the gate. Continue on down and across the lawns to the **Castel Nuovo** (see pp14–15). Your visit here should include the views from the parapets.

Finally, head up **Via Medina** to the **Caffetteria Medina** (see p93), where you can enjoy a drink while admiring the Fountain of Neptune.

See map on p86 ←

Performing Arts Venues

1 Associazione Scarlatti
MAP L5 ▪ Piazza dei Martiri 58
▪ 081 40 60 11 ▪ www.associazione
scarlatti.it

The best of Naples' small musical companies, it hosts classical chamber music and the occasional jazz group. A typical evening might feature the music of Debussy, Ravel, Chausson and Frank. Venues change frequently.

2 Augusteo
MAP L5 ▪ Piazzetta Augusteo
▪ 081 41 42 43 ▪ www.teatro
augusteo.it

Musical comedies are a speciality at this theatre. It also offers shows outside the usual season of October to May. Come here to see contemporary productions, in line with the centuries-old tradition of comic theatre in Naples.

3 Galleria Toledo
MAP M4 ▪ Via Concezione a
Montecalvario 36 ▪ 081 42 50 37
▪ www.galleriatoledo.info

This modern theatre offers avant-garde local works and new international fringe and experimental plays, translated into Italian.

4 Mercadante
MAP N5 ▪ Piazza Municipio 1
▪ 081 551 33 96/03 36 ▪ www.teatro
stabilenapoli.it

Opened in 1779, this historic theatre hosts productions touring Italy.

5 Politeama
MAP M6 ▪ Via Monte di Dio 80
▪ 081 764 50 01 ▪ www.teatro
politeama.it

This large, modern space offers productions of international music, dance and drama. Performers have included German dancer Pina Bausch and US composer Philip Glass.

6 San Carluccio
MAP K6 ▪ Via S Pasquale a
Chiaia 49 ▪ 081 410 44 67

Small companies gravitate here, alternating with cabaret shows.

7 Teatro Nuovo
MAP M4 ▪ Via Concezione a
Montecalvario 16 ▪ 081 497 62 67
▪ www.teatronuovonapoli.it

Fringe, experimental and the best of new international theatre is the keynote at this theatre.

8 Centro di Musica Antica Pieta de' Turchini
MAP M5 ▪ Via S Caterina da Siena 38
▪ 081 40 23 95 ▪ www.turchini.it

In a deconsecrated Baroque church, the Orchestra Cappella della Pieta de' Turchini performs classical music of mostly Neapolitan composers.

9 Teatro Bellini
MAP N2 ▪ Via Conte di Ruvo
14-19 ▪ 081 949 12 66 ▪ www.teatro
bellini.it

Bellini offers mainstream theatre, as well as international and local musicals and concerts. Productions have included *Fiddler on the Roof* and Prokofiev's *Romeo and Juliet*.

Gold and red triumphs, Teatro Bellini

10 Sannazaro
MAP M5 ▪ Via Chiaia 157
▪ 081 41 17 23/ 081 41 88 24
▪ www.teatrosannazaro.it

This lovely theatre dating from 1874 features its own company, often performing works in Neapolitan dialect.

Shopping

Books and prints for sale at Bowinkel

1 Bowinkel
MAP L6 ▪ Via S Lucia 25

One of Naples' finest dealers in old books and prints. Expect to find Italian prints that are centuries-old as well as more modern ones, and a host of other Neapolitan memorabilia.

2 Penna & Carta 1989
MAP K5 ▪ Largo Vasto a Chiaia 86

Come to this pleasant shop for art supplies, fine handmade stationery and top-quality fountain pens, including a selection of decorative hand-blown glass pens.

3 La Murrina
MAP N5 ▪ Via S Carlo 18

These elegant rooms are filled with fine Murano glass, in all shapes, sizes and colours. Exquisite vases, bowls and paperweights.

4 Fusaro
MAP M5 ▪ Via dei Mille 91 & Via Toledo 276

This local chain specializes in designer gear for men – shoes, suits, shirts and ties, jeans and jackets, as well as caps, bags and belts.

5 Maffei
MAP L6 ▪ Via Sta Caterina a Chiaia 10–11

Stylish jewellery at affordable prices. Silver and gold are featured, with an emphasis on modern pieces compatible with today's taste. There are some original lines by local artisans available.

6 Maison d'Art
MAP L6 ▪ Piazza dei Martiri 18

Maison d'Art is one of the best antiques shops in the city – it's rather like browsing through a museum. Real treasures are on display, including 19th-century gouaches of Neapolitan panoramas, 17th-century ceramics and 16th-century bronze candlesticks. Prices are high.

7 Fratelli Tramontano
MAP M5 ▪ Via Chiaia 142

Italians are known the world over for their leather goods, including bags and shoes. Traditional Neapolitan craftsmanship is the byword here.

8 Rino Corcione
MAP L3 ▪ Piazzale S Martino 14–11

This is one of several coral and cameo shops on and near this beautiful piazza. Rino Coricione boasts a vast selection of pieces, some at highly affordable prices.

9 La Bottega della Ceramica
MAP L6 ▪ Via Carlo Poerio 40

The south of Italy is known for its hand-painted ceramics. A host of traditional designs are featured here, from simple earthenware beakers to decorative plates with complex scenes.

10 Dolce & Amaro
MAP M5 ▪ Via Chiaia 160

Thirty-five types of chocolate await you here. Treats include *limoncello*-flavoured dark chocolate and chocolate Neapolitan landmarks, such as Vesuvius. Or how about an all-chocolate coffee-maker with all-chocolate cups?

See map on p86

Nightlife

1 **Al Barcadero**
MAP N6 ■ Banchina Santa Lucia 2 ■ Open May–Sep

This bar captures the charm of the Santa Lucia quarter, immortalized in one of the most famous Neapolitan songs. By the water, near Castel dell'Ovo, it's great for hanging out and enjoying the views.

2 **Vanilla Café**
Via Partenope 12

Perfectly situated on the seashore, this trendy bar-café offers great views of the Bay of Naples. Large crowds flock in for its famous aperitifs, especially during summer, adding to the lively vibe.

3 **Ex Ess**
MAP K5 ■ Via Giuseppe Martucci 28 ■ Closed Mon

Located in one of the city's most elegant and cosmopolitan areas is this friendly underground bar spread across several small rooms. There is live music until midnight.

4 **S'move**
MAP L6 ■ Vico dei Sospiri 10A ■ Closed Aug

Another chic venue, but less pretentious. Although there's no dance floor, the good selection of music keeps things moving.

The bar at S'move

5 **Enoteca Belledonne**
MAP L6 ■ Vico Belledonne a Chiaia 18 ■ Closed Sun

Shelves of wine bottles lining the walls and a rustic decor provide the perfect backdrop for this elegant wine bar. An extensive wine list and light fare is on offer.

6 **66 Fusion Bar**
MAP L6 ■ Via Bisignano 58

With an impressively stocked bar, this nightlife spot in Chiaia is popular with locals for its inventive cocktails and lively atmosphere. Excellent wines are available and there is an outdoor seating area.

7 **Around Midnight**
MAP K3 ■ Via G Bonito 32A

This live jazz venue focuses on standards and classics most of the time, booking well-known performers from around Italy.

8 **Macho Lato**
MAP K1 ■ Via Abate Minichini 62

Attracting an open-minded and diverse gay crowd, this club offers two levels with dancing, lounging and entertainment. Cover charge.

9 **Ba-Bar**
MAP L6 ■ Via Bisignano 20

For an elegant evening out, head to the stylish Chiaia neighbourhood where locals go for an evening *aperitivo* or dinner and drinks. The French bistro atmosphere, friendly service, extensive wine list and international beer selection make this lively night spot stand out.

10 **Discoteca il Fico**
MAP K2 ■ Via Tasso 466

A villa dating from the 1800s is the fine setting for this chic disco bar. During the summer months when the weather is fine, the scene moves outdoors to the terrace from where there are great views of the Bay of Naples and Mount Vesuvius.

Places to Eat

1 **Caffè Gambrinus**
MAP M5 ▪ Via Chiaia 1–2 ▪ €€

This *belle époque* institution still retains much of its original decor. Popular with free-thinking intellectuals and writers, it was closed down by the Fascists as a result. The pastries and buffet lunch are good.

Elegant dining at Caffè Gambrinus

2 **Caffetteria Medina**
MAP P4 ▪ Via Medina 30–31 ▪ €€

The café's main claim to fame is its location right next to the Neptune Fountain. Tables outside provide you with an excellent vantage point.

3 **Pintauro**
MAP N4 ▪ Via Toledo 275 ▪ €

This traditional *pasticceria* (pastry shop) is an ideal choice for procuring the signature Neapolitan sweets, such as *sfogliatella* and *babà (see p67)*.

4 **Pinterré**
MAP K2 ▪ Via Partenope 12 ▪ €

This seaside café is a great place for kicking back and watching the world go by, plus it offers some of the city's most captivating views.

5 **Brandi**
MAP M5 ▪ Salita Sant'Anna di Palazzo 1 ▪ 081 41 69 28 ▪ €€

A Naples institution, laying claim to having invented the pizza margherita during a visit from Italy's Queen Margherita in 1889. Full restaurant menu, too. Reservations essential.

PRICE CATEGORIES
For a three-course meal for one with half a bottle of wine (or equivalent meal), taxes and extra charges.
....
€ under €30   €€ €30–€50   €€€ over €50

6 **Gastronomia LUISE**
MAP M4 ▪ Via Toledo 266 ▪ 081 41 53 67 ▪ No credit cards ▪ €

A small deli offering local fried food delights such as *pizza fritta*, *arancini* (fried rice balls) and a selection of tempting pasta and meat dishes.

7 **'a Taverna 'e zi Carmela**
MAP L6 ▪ Via Niccolò Tommaseo 11–12 ▪ Closed Sun ▪ €€

This family-run place has lots of charm. The speciality is seafood.

8 **Rosati**
MAP M4 ▪ Via Chiaia 260 ▪ 081 42 16 86 ▪ €€

An elegant restaurant and *pizzeria* that serves traditional Neapolitan cuisine at lunchtime.

Pizza from Rosati

9 **Osteria da Tonino**
MAP K5 ▪ Via Sta Teresa a Chiaia 47 ▪ 081 42 15 33 ▪ Closed Sun, Aug ▪ No credit cards ▪ €€

Excellent dishes here include seafood stew. Always lively.

10 **Chalet Ciro**
MAP K2 ▪ Via F Caracciolo, by Largo Sermoneta, Mergellina ▪ 081 66 99 28 ▪ No credit cards ▪ €€

Excellent seafood and pasta combinations draw a loyal following.

See map on p86

🔟 Vesuvius and Around

Few places on earth are as awe-inspiring as this area of southern Italy. Here lies the archetypal heart of Campania, where high culture and the indifferent violence of nature have met again and again. Although many lost their families, homes and lives, mankind has ironically gained from these deadly encounters with the mighty volcano that is Mount Vesuvius – in the very act of destruction entire

cultures have been preserved for posterity. Here is the city of Pompeii, the town of Herculaneum, and other amazing villas – all of them replete with art and architecture that reveal to us the great heritage of beauty bequeathed by our forebears from Roman times. In later centuries, the unearthing of these treasures inspired even kings to build sumptuous palaces, so that they could sample firsthand the exciting discoveries.

Roman mosaic, Herculaneum

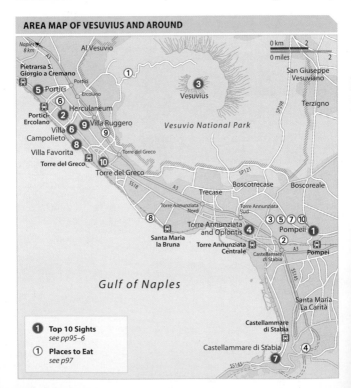

AREA MAP OF VESUVIUS AND AROUND

1 **Top 10 Sights**
see pp95–6

① **Places to Eat**
see p97

The ancient city of Pompeii in the shadow of Mount Vesuvius

1 Pompeii

Certainly no archaeological find is more important than that of ancient Pompeii, where a culture was captured forever by the eruption of Mount Vesuvius in AD 79. Not only can we see the streets, buildings, furnishings, art, tools, jewellery, and even the food and drink of the people who lived here, but plaster casts reveal the people themselves. From the ruling class down to slaves, we can see their last moments during those terrible few hours that doomed the city *(see pp30–31)*.

2 Herculaneum

This town, largely a resort in ancient times located right on the sea, was also buried alive by mud and lava from Vesuvius. The resulting preservation is, if anything, even better, bringing down to us wooden structures and other more perishable materials. However the excavations began in the 18th century when the science of archaeology had yet to be developed, so diggers were not very careful, being mostly on a royal treasure hunt for statuary, mosaics and fresco paintings *(see pp32–3)*.

3 Vesuvius

MAP D3 ■ **Guided walks daily**
■ **Adm** ■ **www.vesuvioexpress.info**

Continental Europe's only active volcano has not blown up since its last rumble in 1944, but experts say it could happen at any time; an invigorating hike around the crater is certainly a memorable experience. Drive to the parking area near the top of the volcano, from where the 1.5-hour return trail is accompanied by volcanologist guides, except in bad weather *(see p31)*.

4 Torre Annunziata and Oplontis

Few places present such a stark contrast to the visitor as this one. The contemporary squalor of uncontrolled urban blight hides, within its depressed grime, imperial splendours of the ancient world. The town is infamous these days for its crime and poverty, yet just two blocks from the train station lie the beautifully preserved ruins of one of the most sumptuous villas to have been preserved by Vesuvius's eruption *(see pp32–3)*.

Villa Sabina Poppaea, Oplontis

⑤ Reggia di Portici and the Vesuvian Villas

MAP L2 ■ Reggia di Portici, Via Università 100 ■ Open 8:30am–7pm Mon–Fri (park & chapel only) ■ Guided tours: Reggia (081 775 48 50), Villas (081 732 21 34) ■ Adm (chapel free)

The Vesuvian Villas were begun by King Charles III and Queen Maria in the 18th century. His Reggia (palace), designed by Antonio Medrano, was the first and greatest, the rest of which were built by other members of the Bourbon court. For the most part the villas are now dilapidated.

⑥ Villa Campolieto

MAP L2 ■ Corso Resina 283, Ercolano ■ Open 10am–1pm Tue–Sun ■ Guided tours ■ Adm

This stupendous villa was designed by the Vanvitelli brothers between 1760–75. It features a circular portico, where concerts are held, and enjoys a lovely panorama of the bay. Some of the rooms have been restored to their original decor, while others are used for special exhibitions.

⑦ Castellammare di Stabia

This port town has been known since ancient times for its thermal springs – the many different waters are each thought to be therapeutic in specific ways. As with its neighbours, its beauty has been compromised by poverty and developers, but it is not without charm. Nearby, the ruins of aristocratic villas, Arianna and San Marco, offer glimpses into wealthy lifestyles of 2,000 years ago *(see p33)*.

Castellammare di Stabia

THE GOLDEN MILE

The 18th-century evolution of *Il Miglio d'Oro* can be traced back to Maria Amalia Cristina, Queen of Naples (below). She had grown up in a Viennese palace adorned with two marble statues unearthed at Herculaneum. When she arrived in Naples, she wanted a palace near the site. It started a trend among the nobility and some 120 villas were built.

⑧ Villa Favorita

MAP L2 ■ Corso Resina 291, Ercolano ■ 081 192 44 532 ■ Open 10am–1pm Tue–Sun

Villa Favorita was boarded up at least 100 years ago – with Italian Unification the noble homes became an obsolete symbol of decadence. However the park and the annexe are open to visitors, the former punctuated with pavilions.

⑨ Villa Ruggero

MAP L2 ■ Via A Rossi 40, Ercolano ■ Open 10am–1pm Tue–Sun

Set back from the sea, this house was built for the Baronial Petti family. It has been restored, with Rococo decorations, frescoes and marble busts.

⑩ Torre del Greco

MAP L3

This town has been home to coral and cameo artisans for centuries, a craft that still draws admirers today. Yet its rough streets are among the area's worst for violent crime, and it lies in the line of fire from Vesuvius, last suffering destruction in 1794.

Places to Eat

PRICE CATEGORIES

For a three-course meal for one with half a bottle of wine (or equivalent meal), taxes and extra charges.

€ under €30 €€ €30–€50 €€€ over €50

1 Kona, Ercolano

MAP L2 ■ Via Osservatorio 14 ■ 081 777 39 68 ■ Closed D daily, except Sat evening ■ €€

Surrounded by gardens and with a view of the Gulf of Naples from the terrace, dining here is a tranquil experience. Seafood specialities and traditional pasta dishes make up the menu; the fresh seafood salad comes recommended.

2 Ristorante Suisse, Pompei
MAP E4 ■ Piazza Porta Marina Inferiore ■ 081 862 25 36 ■ €€

Of all the eateries outside the main gate of the ruins, this one offers the nicest atmosphere. It has indoor and outside tables, and serves a good standard of *trattoria* fare.

3 Zi Caterina, Pompei
MAP E4 ■ Via Roma 20 ■ 081 850 74 47 ■ €€

Seafood is a speciality here; try *seppie con finocchi e olive* (cuttlefish with fennel and olives). The wine list features local vintages.

4 Grand Hotel La Medusa, Castellammare di Stabia
MAP E4 ■ Via Passeggiata Archeologica 5 ■ 081 872 33 83 ■ €€

This elegant hotel has a large dining room offering set meals, as well as *à la carte* selections.

5 Nuovo Ristorante Anfiteatro, Pompei
MAP E4 ■ Via Plinio 9 ■ 081 850 60 42 ■ Closed Fri ■ €€

Located immediately outside the excavations, this restaurant has been running since 1922. The fresh fish is a good choice in summer.

6 Bar degli Amorini, Ercolano

MAP L2 ■ Corso Resina ■ No credit cards ■ €

Enjoy a simple meal and the chilled red wine, made on the premises.

7 Il Principe, Pompei
MAP E4 ■ Piazza B Longo 8 ■ 081 850 55 66 ■ Closed Sun & Mon ■ €€€

Elegant decor is graced with reproductions of Pompeian art, and the cuisine also takes its inspiration from ancient sources. Classical writers have provided recipes that have been adapted to modern tastes, earning the proprietors a Michelin star. The on-site wine bar also serves food.

Il Principe, Pompei

8 Casa Rossa 1888, Torre del Greco
MAP D3 ■ Via Vesuvio 30 ■ 081 883 15 49 ■ Closed Tue ■ €€

Good Neapolitan food right on the beach with fine views of the bay.

9 La Mammola, Torre del Greco
MAP L2 ■ Hotel Marad, Via S Sebastiano 24 ■ 081 849 21 68 ■ €€

A beautiful restaurant serving traditional cuisine with creative flair.

10 Al Gamberone, Pompei
MAP E4 ■ Via Piave 36 ■ 081 850 68 14 ■ Closed Tue ■ €€

Dining alfresco under the lemon and orange trees is a treat. Seafood is key.

See map on p94

TOP 10 The Islands, Sorrento and the South

This is one of the world's most intensely emotive zones, where verdant-crowned cliffs plunge into the blue sea. On these islands is where the Greeks first brought their high culture to the area, where Roman emperors lived in stupendous luxury, and where, in more recent times, the world's most glamorous celebrities indulged in their own lavish lifestyles. When the American writer John Steinbeck first saw the Amalfi Coast he was moved to uncontrollable weeping. He was not the first – nor will he be the last – to succumb to the emotional impact of the area's potent beauty.

Forio town on the cliffs of the island of Ischia

AREA MAP OF THE ISLANDS, SORRENTO AND THE SOUTH

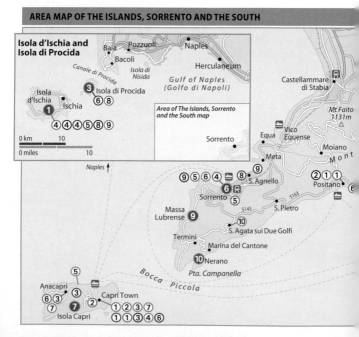

Previous pages Rowing boats on the shore at Cetara, Amalfi Coast

1 Ischia
MAP B4

The island of Ischia is surmounted by an extinct 788-m (2,585-ft) volcano, Monte Epomeo, and the many hot mineral springs here (some of them radioactive) have drawn cure- and pleasure-seekers to their soothing sources since ancient times. Green and rugged in appearance, the island also benefits from fine, long beaches. Like Capri, Ischia has had its share of famous residents – in the 19th century the Norwegian playwright Henrik Ibsen wrote *Peer Gynt* during a stay here, while in the 20th century the English poet W.H. Auden and his homosexual circle scandalized the locals. The island was also the first place in the area to be colonized by the Greeks, in the 8th century BC.

2 Paestum

These ancient Greek temples are among the most complete – and most evocative – to have survived into modern times, even taking into

Remains of a Greek temple, Paestum

account those in Greece itself. Besides the beauty and majesty of these timeless structures, this site has offered up countless other treasures, the remains of the Greco-Roman city that thrived here for some 1,000 years. The wonderful on-site museum is the repository of many unique finds, including the only known Greek paintings to have survived the ages. Taken from a tomb found nearby, the frescoes include a depiction of a joyous banquet of lovers, and a renowned diver – possibly a metaphor for the Greek conception of the afterlife *(see pp38–9)*.

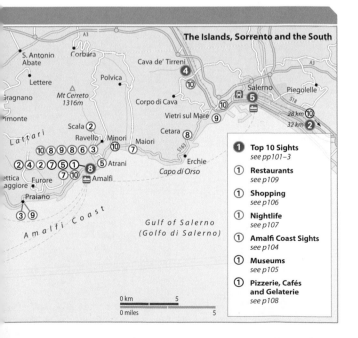

The Islands, Sorrento and the South

S. Antonio Abate
Corbara
Cava de' Tirreni
Lettere
Polvica
Gragnano
Mt Cerreto 1316m
Corpo di Cava
Salerno
Piegolelle
Imonte
Scala
Vietri sul Mare
Latṭari
Ravello
Minori
Maiori
Cetara
28 km
32 km
Scala
Atrani
Erchie
Furore
Amalfi
Capo d'Orso
ettica
aggiore
Praiano
Gulf of Salerno
(Golfo di Salerno)
Amalfi Coast

1	**Top 10 Sights** *see pp101–3*
1	**Restaurants** *see p109*
1	**Shopping** *see p106*
1	**Nightlife** *see p107*
1	**Amalfi Coast Sights** *see p104*
1	**Museums** *see p105*
1	**Pizzerie, Cafés and Gelaterie** *see p108*

0 km   5
0 miles   5

3 Procida
MAP B4

Smaller than Capri and Ischia and much less touristy, Procida attracts holiday-makers looking for tranquillity and cultural tradition. The island is flat with highly fertile soil, and is noted for its lemons, considered the best in the region. The island's most original feature, however, is its unique architecture. The colourful houses along the Chiaiolella Port, Marina Corricella and Marina di Sancin Cattolico are known for their vaults – built as winter boat shelters – arches and external staircases.

Colourful buildings, Procida

4 Cava de' Tirreni
MAP F4 ■ Abbey: Open 8:30am–noon, 4–5:30pm daily; must be booked

In a mountainous valley north of the Amalfi Coast, this undiscovered town was put up in the Middle Ages thanks to the Benedictine abbey Badia della Santissima Trinità (Abbey of the Holy Trinity) founded in 1011. A visit to the abbey and the medieval Borgo Scacciaventi in the town's centre is an evocative walk through time.

5 Salerno
MAP F4 ■ Duomo: Piazza Alfano I ■ Open 9am–1pm, 4–6pm daily

Renowned in medieval times for its medical school, this city has been almost ignored by tourism; that may change now that the historic centre has undergone a restoration. The Romanesque Duomo is a reminder that Salerno was the capital of southern Italy in the 11th century.

HIKING SPOTS

This region retains a great deal of virtually untouched natural beauty. On Capri, one of the best hikes is up the Scala Fenicia to Anacapri and then on up to the top, Monte Solaro. On Ischia, head up Via Monterone or Via Bocca from Forio, through the Falanga Forest to the summit of Monte Epomeo. Along the Amalfi Coast, the Sentieri degli Dei, above Positano, from Montepertuso to Nocella, offers stupendous views.

6 Sorrento
MAP D5

Palisades and grand hotels notwithstanding, there is no getting around the fact that Sorrento can be chaotic. Yet the town has been a resort since the 1700s – Casanova and Goethe are two notable past visitors – and there is certainly plenty of charm to be found in the old streets.

7 Capri
The fabled isle has had its detractors – it has been called "nothing more than a rocky cliff with over-priced cafés" – and, in ancient times, the notorious shenanigans of Tiberius gave it an enduring reputation as the ultimate in decadence, as did the party life here in the 1950s. Yet, if you choose to stay awhile, you will discover the real Capri beyond the hype – a world of traditional farm life, scenic hiking terrain and sparkling azure waters for swimming and boating. A place with undeniable allure *(see pp34–5)*.

Faraglioni rocks, Capri

8 The Amalfi Coast
MAP E5

The famed Costiera Amalfitana lives up to the highest expectations. The winding corniche road offers striking panoramas, and some of the towns seem to defy gravity, clinging to steep slopes. Beauty and history are everywhere, with the most popular destinations being the towns of Amalfi, Positano and Ravello *(see pp36–7)*. The beaches are rocky yet undeniably beautiful, and time spent discovering this perpendicular paradise never fails to delight.

The town of Amalfi, Amalfi Coast

9 Massa Lubrense
MAP D5

To the west of Sorrento, this is one of several fishing villages clustered around little ports. Rarely crowded, the site affords wonderful views across to Capri from the belvedere in Largo Vescovado. At Marina di Lobra there's a beach.

10 Nerano
MAP D5

This quiet fishing village, close to the tip of the peninsula, offers a peaceful escape. While administratively part of Massa Lubrense on the northern side of the peninsula, its remote location on the southern side means fine views and a scenic beach in the seaside hamlet of Marina del Cantone. With an atmospheric setting, sophisticated seaside dining, and fine hiking along the rugged coastline, including the protected nature reserve at Punta Campanella, it's a lovely spot to while away an afternoon on the Amalfi Coast.

A DAY'S ISLAND HOPPING

▶ MORNING

The tour begins on the island of **Procida**. To get there, take either the first hydrofoil from Naples-Beverello or Naples-Mergellina or the first ferry from Pozzuoli, all of which take about 35 minutes. You will arrive at Marina Grande, greeted by the sight of fishing boats and the colourful houses lining the port. Take a quick hike to the island's highest point, the **Terra Murata** ("walled town").

Back down on the marina, enjoy some refreshment at **Bar Capriccio** *(Via Roma 99)* while waiting for your hydrofoil to Ischia *(see p101)*.

On Ischia you will arrive at **Casamicciola**, the island's second port, where you can have lunch (Fri–Sun) at the wonderfully rustic **Il Focolare** *(Via Cretaio 68)*.

AFTERNOON

After lunch take a tour around the island in a glass-bottom boat (departs 2:30pm), stopping at the town of **Sant'Angelo**. Here you can take in the views, lounge by the dockside or walk along the cliff above **Maronti Beach**.

At the end of your tour, you can opt to stay over in one of the hotels in Casamicciola, or take a hydrofoil back to the mainland. If you spend the night, the next morning take the hydrofoil or one of the ferries to **Capri** *(see pp34–5)*. After riding the funicular up to Capri Town, follow the signs up to the ruins of Villa Jovis for the breathtaking views.

See map on pp100–1

Amalfi Coast Sights

Positano, climbing up the hillside

 Positano
Known for decades as a playground for the rich and famous, this is an astonishingly vertical town in shades of pink and other faded pastels. Only one street snakes its way through the village – the only way to reach the beach and the heart of the village is to take the steps down (see pp36–7).

 Scala
MAP E5
This lesser-known, tranquil village sits across the valley from Ravello. Indeed, the best view of Ravello is from Scala, which is also the starting point for hikes to Amalfi and the Valle delle Ferriere (see pp36–7).

3 Praiano
MAP E5 ▪ Grotta dello Smeraldo: Open Apr–Oct: 9am–4pm daily, Nov–Mar: 9am–3pm daily; Adm ▪ 089 87 31 90 (boat trips)
This little fishing village is perched on a ridge. Further along, you come to the Grotta dello Smeraldo (Emerald Cave). A lift takes you down to the boats to enter the grotto. The cave is also accessible by boat from Amalfi.

4 Amalfi
Amalfi is the largest and most historic town on its eponymous coastline. Between the 9th and 12th centuries the republic was at its height of mercantile power and the architecture still evokes that glory. The Duomo (cathedral) is glorious (see pp36–7).

 Atrani
MAP E5
▪ San Salvatore de' Bireto
This little town exudes a quiet charm, with its arcades and a maze of alley-stairways. Amalfi's doges received their investiture at its church, San Salvatore de' Bireto.

6 Ravello
In the 13th century Ravello was an important player in the sea trade and the medieval look accounts for its captivating beauty (see pp36–7).

 Minori and Maiori
MAP E5
Maiori has the coast's longest beach, while Minori has the archaeological site, the Villa Romana (see p105).

8 Cetara
MAP F4
Home to the coast's most active fishing fleet, it is also the place to buy colatura di alici, a fish sauce descended from the ancient Roman one called garum. A tuna festival takes place every year in July.

9 Vietri sul Mare
MAP F4
Vietri is universally known for its ceramics, which begun in the 1400s and are still masterly handcrafted and hand-painted.

10 Conca dei Marini
MAP E5
Known for the luminous light at the Grotta dello Smeraldo (Emerald Grotto), but linger a little longer to see the picturesque marina, 16th-century watchtower and views from the San Pancrazio Church.

Museums

1 Certosa di San Giacomo, Capri

MAP U2 ■ Viale Certosa ■ 081 837 62 18 ■ Open 9am–2pm Tue–Sun

This 14th-century monastery features North African-style vaults forming a series of little domes. It now houses the town's library.

2 Arsenale Museum, Amalfi

MAP E5 ■ Largo Cesareo Console 3 ■ 089 87 11 70/ 339 150 58 18 ■ Open 10am–7pm daily ■ Adm

Set in Amalfi's medieval arsenal, this small museum traces the history of the powerful Republic of Amalfi and its contributions to the development of the compass and maritime laws.

3 Villa San Michele, Anacapri

MAP S1 ■ 081 837 14 01 ■ Open Mar: 9am–6pm; Apr & Oct: 9am–5pm; May–Sep: 9am–6pm; Nov–Feb: 9am–3:30pm ■ Adm

This villa contains ancient marbles and furnishings from the 17th to 19th centuries (see p35).

Ancient statues at Villa San Michele

4 Castello Aragonese, Ischia

MAP B4 ■ 081 99 28 34 ■ Open Mar–Nov: 9am–7:30pm ■ Adm

In the 16th century poetess Vittoria Colonna held court here, making Ischia the cultural centre of the Mediterranean. Part of the ruin is now the Il Monastero hotel (see p131).

5 Area Archeologica de Santa Restituta, Ischia

MAP A4 ■ Piazza Santa Restituta, Lacco Ameno ■ Open 9:30am–12:30pm Mon–Sat ■ Adm

Sitting below the 19th-century church are the remains of a 4th-century Christian basilica.

6 Abbazia di San Michele Arcangelo, Procida

MAP B4 ■ Via Terra Murata 89 ■ 081 896 76 12 ■ Open 10am–12:45pm Mon, 10am–12:45pm, 3–5:30pm Tue–Sat

Overlooking the sea, this 11th-century abbey is notable for its paintings by pupils of Luca Giordano.

7 Museo Antiquarium Equano, Vico Equense

MAP D4 ■ Casa Municipale, Via Filangieri 98 ■ Open 9am–1pm Mon–Fri

Finds from this Roman town consist of pottery, figurines and tools. They are now housed in the Town Hall.

8 Correale di Terranova, Sorrento

MAP D5 ■ Via Correale 50 ■ 081 878 18 46 ■ timings vary, check website ■ Adm ■ www.museocorreale.it

In this 18th-century villa, archaeological finds include a 4th-century BC Greek original of Artemis on a Deer.

9 Museo Archeologico Georges Vallet, Piano di Sorrento

MAP D5 ■ Via Ripa di Cassano 14 ■ 081 532 14 78 ■ Open 9am–7pm Tue–Sun

This interesting museum boasts finds from all over the peninsula, including pottery and weapons.

10 Villa Romana, Minori

MAP E5 ■ Via Capodipiazza 28 ■ Open 9am–1 hour before sunset

In this aristocratic villa the fresco style dates from the 1st century AD. Artifacts excavated here and nearby are also displayed.

See map on pp100–1 ←

Shopping

1 Sandalmakers, Capri
Canfora: MAP T1; Via Camerelle 3 ■ L'Arte del Sandal Caprese di Antonio Viva: MAP U1; Via G Orlandi 75, Anacapri

Cobblers jollier than these would be hard to find. Stop by to pick out designs you like and within a few hours – unless you choose something extra fancy – you'll have your hand-tooled, made-to-measure sandals.

Carthusia on Capri

2 Carthusia, Capri
MAP C5 ■ Via Camerelle 10

The closest you can come to bringing the natural beauty of Capri home is with Carthusia's collection of perfumes inspired by and created on Capri. Fragrances, soaps and home scents make beautiful gifts.

3 Corallium, Anacapri
MAP T1 ■ Via G Orlandi 163–5

A coral and cameo factory in Ercolano. The selection is extraordinary, created with both silver and gold, and prices are excellent. A certificate of guarantee comes with every purchase.

4 Limonoro, Sorrento
MAP D5 ■ Via S Cesareo 51

One of the top souvenirs from the area is *limoncello*, the signature lemon liqueur. This is a good place to watch it being made, after

which you'll understand why it packs such a punch – it's basically pure alcohol with flavouring.

5 Salvatore Gargiulo, Sorrento
MAP D5 ■ Via Fuoro 33

Examples of Sorrentine *intarsia* (marquetry) are to be seen all over town, but this workshop turns out top-quality products at reasonable prices. Note the music boxes.

6 La Galleria dell'Arte, Anacapri
MAP T1 ■ Via G Orlandi 107

Some of the best ceramics on the island. Designs tend to evoke the natural hues of the setting – azure, gold, green – usually with flowers and vines or other florid vegetation. Anything can be designed to your specifications and you can watch the artists at work.

7 La Scuderia del Duca, Amalfi
MAP E5 ■ Cesareo Console 8

Amalfi's handmade paper-making tradition is vibrantly on display in this beautiful shop.

8 Camo, Ravello
MAP E4 ■ Piazza Vesovado 6

A cameo factory (and museum) that sells cameos and coral jewellery.

9 Ceramiche d'Arte, Ravello
MAP E4 ■ Via della Repubblica 41

This workshop is the place to come for gorgeous ceramics decorated with traditional designs.

10 Milleunaceramica, Amalfi
MAP E5 ■ Via Pietro Capuano 36

This shop is a treasure trove of locally produced ceramics. Each piece is handpicked by the owner and created by artisans.

Milleunaceramica

Nightlife

 Taverna Anema e Core, Capri
MAP U1 ▪ Via Sella Orta 1 ▪ Closed Oct–Mar: Mon–Fri

The "Soul and Heart" taverna is still redolent of *la dolce vita* vibes of decades past and is considered Capri's premier nightclub. It attracts a chic, yet fun-loving crowd.

② Number Two, Capri
MAP U1 ▪ Via Camerelle 1

Another hot spot and local celebrity hangout. The DJ spins cool house and techno dance music, but don't get here before 2am. Dressy club attire is *de rigueur.*

③ Qubè Café, Capri
MAP C5 ▪ Via li Curti 6

A quirky disco-bar a short stroll from Capri's stylish Piazzetta. With a local feel that's a refreshing change from the island's posh night spots, music varies from classic rock to electronic.

④ Discoteca Valentino Pianobar, Ischia
MAP B4 ▪ Corso Vittoria Colonna 97

This beautifully decorated club attracts a young, energetic crowd.

⑤ Chaplin's Pub, Sorrento
MAP D5 ▪ Corso Italia 18

A delightful mix of Irish and Italian, this friendly, family-owned Irish pub in the heart of Sorrento offers an excellent beer selection.

⑥ Music on the Rocks, Positano
MAP E5 ▪ Grotta dell'Incanto 51 ▪ Closed winter

Evocatively set inside a cavern, this beachside disco pub is the hot spot for nightlife on the Amalfi Coast. At weekends it is a high-energy nightclub featuring international DJs and live music. Cover charge.

La Piazzetta, the social heart of Capri

⑦ La Piazzetta, Capri
MAP U1

Capri Town's main square may be small but it's big on *la vita mondana* (sophisticated lifestyle). The little bars, with their cluster of outdoor tables, are a magnet for daytrippers and locals alike, although the latter generally turn up after dark when the former have moved on.

⑧ Annunziata Church, Ravello
MAP E4 ▪ Via della Annunziata ▪ www.ravelloarts.org

Dating from the Middle Ages, this church is no longer used for religious services; the Ravello Concert Society presents year-round chamber concerts in this evocative setting.

⑨ Africana, Marina di Praia
MAP E5

The approach to this disco is via a walkway cut out of a seafront rock face, while the dance floor seems to be suspended above the waves. Decor includes ethnic masks and parrots.

⑩ Villa Rufolo, Ravello
MAP E4 ▪ Piazza Duomo ▪ Open 8am–8pm in summer, 9am–4pm in winter

Jazz concerts and classical recitals are held in the grounds of the Villa Rufolo from March to November.

See map on pp100–1 ←

Pizzerie, Cafés and Gelaterie

① Gran Caffè, Amalfi

MAP E5 ■ Corso delle Repubbliche Marinare 37/38 ■ €

With picturesque outdoor seating overlooking the beach and port of Amalfi, this café is a popular spot with locals and visitors for enjoying drinks or a light meal. The sunset views are spectacular.

Relaxing on the piazza outside Pasticceria Pansa

② La Zagara, Positano

MAP E5 ■ Via dei Mulini 4–8 ■ €

La Zagara is a major tourist magnet, but there's no denying that the treats they turn out here are delicious: pastries, cakes, fresh fruit sorbets and the like. The patio, with fragrant lemon trees, is captivating.

③ Bar Tiberio, Capri

MAP U1 ■ La Piazzetta ■ €

One of the main bars on the Piazzetta, but everyone has his or her own favourite. Great for people-watching.

④ Bar Calise, Ischia

MAP B4 ■ Piazza degli Eroi 69 ■ €

One of the island's best bars, with excellent *gelato* (ice cream) and *dolci* (desserts). It's surrounded by dense greenery in the middle of a traffic circle in this laid-back port.

⑤ Da Maria, Amalfi

MAP E5 ■ Via Lorenzo d'Amalfi 14 ■ 089 87 18 80 ■ Closed Mon ■ €

Amalfi's best wood-fired pizza can be found at this friendly place near Piazza Duomo. Local specialities also feature on the menu.

⑥ Villa Verde, Capri

MAP U1 ■ Via Sella Orta 6/a ■ 081 837 70 24 ■ €€

Offering spacious indoor seating as well as a lush garden, this restaurant has exquisite *focaccia* and pizza and an excellent house red from Calabria.

⑦ Pasticceria Pansa, Amalfi

MAP E5 ■ Piazza Duomo 40 ■ €

An Amalfi institution since 1830, this elegant bar offers a wide selection of irresistible sweets and locally made chocolates. The chocolate covered citrus peels are a treat. Outdoor tables provide a view of the goings-on in the main square.

⑧ Da Pasquale, Sant'Angelo, Ischia

MAP B4 ■ Via Sant'Angelo 79 ■ 081 90 42 08 ■ €

Dining is home-style here, even to the occasional sharing of tables and bench seating. The pizza is tasty and there's a good choice of beer and wine.

⑨ Sant'Antonino, Sorrento

MAP D5 ■ Via Santa Maria delle Grazie 6 ■ 081 877 12 00 ■ €

Excellent, wood-fired pizza is served here for lunch and dinner. The heat of traditional wood ovens flash-bakes the dough, preventing the toppings from becoming soggy.

⑩ Nonna Sceppa, Paestum

MAP H6 ■ Via Laura 53 ■ 082 885 10 64 ■ Closed Thu (winter only), Oct ■ €€

The least touristy of the choices here is a highly recommended restaurant that turns out excellent pizzas, as well as seafood and other home-style dishes. Wild mushrooms in season – try some on your pizza.

Restaurants

(1) La Cambusa, Positano
MAP E5 ■ Piazza Vespucci 4
■ 089 87 54 32 ■ Closed winter ■ €€

Positioned to the right of the beach, with dining on a porticoed balcony. Seafood is the thing to go for.

(2) Marina Grande, Amalfi
MAP E5 ■ Via della Regione 4
■ 089 87 11 29 ■ €€

One of the best restaurants in town, right on the sea. Dishes include seafood ravioli with *arugula* (rocket) sauce.

(3) Villa Maria, Ravello
MAP E4 ■ Via Santa Chiari 2
■ 089 85 72 55 ■ €€€

With a breathtaking setting and pergola-covered dining terrace, this is a peaceful respite for savouring the views and Ravello specialities.

(4) Buca di Bacco "da Serafina", Capri
MAP U1 ■ Via Longano 25
■ 081 837 07 23 ■ Closed Wed ■ €€

This welcoming place is top of most locals' list, for both quality and price. Cooking features seafood and *antipasti*.

(5) Da Paolino Lemon Trees, Capri
MAP C5 ■ Via Palazzo e Mare 11
■ 081 837 61 02 ■ €€€

Enjoy romantic outdoor dining under the lemon trees at this country-style restaurant. Traditional Caprese dishes are as luscious as the setting.

PRICE CATEGORIES

For a three-course meal for one with half a bottle of wine (or equivalent meal), taxes and extra charges.

€ under €30   €€ €30–€50   €€€ over €50

(6) Terrazza Bosquet, Sorrento
MAP D5 ■ Grand Hotel Excelsior Vittoria, Piazza Tasso 34
■ 081 877 71 11 ■ €€€

The grandest experience Sorrento has to offer, in the frescoed dining room of this superlative hotel. Silver, china, crystal and fine linen complement the service you receive.

(7) Il Solitario, Anacapri
MAP T1 ■ Via G Orlandi 96
■ 081 837 13 82 ■ €

Hidden away down a narrow walkway, this delightful place is like being in someone's private garden. Everything is homemade and the freshest the season has to offer.

(8) La Conchiglia, Chiaia Beach, Procida
MAP B4 ■ Steps from Via Pizzaco 10
■ 081 896 76 02 ■ €€

Get here by walking down 183 steps from Piazza Olmo or reserve a boat trip. Once here, try pasta with sweet mussels and courgettes (zucchini).

(9) Alberto al Mare, Ischia
MAP B4 ■ Via Cristoforo Colombo 8 ■ 081 98 12 59 ■ €€

Located over the water, the bounty of the sea is the speciality here. Options might include swordfish or monkfish.

(10) Don Alfonso 1890, Sant'Agata sui Due Golfi, Sorrentine Peninsula
MAP D5 ■ Corso Sant' Agata 13
■ 081 878 00 26 ■ Closed Mon, 7 Jan–7 Mar ■ €€€

With two Michelin stars expect lavish elegance and impeccable food. The tasting menus and their accompanying wines are superb.

Da Paolino Lemon Trees, Capri

See map on pp100–1 ←

🔟 Posillipo, Pozzuoli and the North

If central seaside Naples is known as "Royal Naples", the coastal area to the west could be called "Imperial Naples" for its enormous popularity with imperial families and their courtiers in ancient Roman times. Significant ruins left by them are everywhere hiding behind the postwar *abusivo* (illegal) building developments that now blot the landscape. However, the area is subject to one of nature's stranger phenomena, called Bradyseism – underground volcanic activity gives rise to "slow earthquakes", resulting in the continual rising and lowering of the land, making it an unstable base for settlement. The region is relatively unexplored by modern-day tourists but was top of the list for those who took the 19th-century Grand Tour, not least because it includes one of Italy's finest palaces, the Reggia di Caserta.

Royal throne, Reggia di Caserta

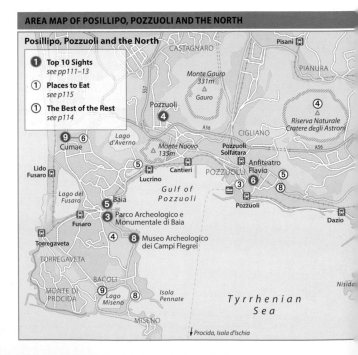

AREA MAP OF POSILLIPO, POZZUOLI AND THE NORTH

Posillipo, Pozzuoli and the North

1 **Top 10 Sights**
see pp111–13

1 **Places to Eat**
see p115

1 **The Best of the Rest**
see p114

View from Parco Virgiliano

① Parco Virgiliano

MAP J2 ■ Salita della Grotta 20
■ 081 410 72 11 ■ Open 9am–4pm
Mon–Sat (to noon in summer)

Occupying the summit of a large hill, this park has amazing views whichever way you turn. Below lies the island of Nisida, formed from an ancient volcanic crater. The tomb of

the epic poet Virgil is said to be here in the ruins of a *columbarium* (sepulchre) used by ancient Romans to house the ashes of the dead.

② Marechiaro

MAP J2

One of the most romantic spots on this evocative coastline, this little fishing village is dotted with ancient ruins and restaurants with great views *(see p61)*. The panoramic vista of Vesuvius from here is repeatedly celebrated, most nostalgically in the quintessential song *'O Sole Mio*.

③ Parco Archeologico e Monumentale di Baia

MAP B3 ■ Via Fusaro 37, Bacoli ■ 081 868 75 92 or 06 399 67 050 to book
■ Open 9am–1 hour before sunset Tue–Sun ■ Adm ■ www.coopculture.it

Arranged in terraces, this excavated area has an ancient spa and a Temple of Diana. The spa complex comprises baths named after Venus and Mercury, the latter a large swimming pool once covered with a dome.

④ Pozzuoli

MAP C3

Called Puteoli by the Romans, this seaside town was a major player 2,000 years ago. Ruins here include the archaeological site of Rione Terra, and the Serapeum, thought for centuries to be a temple of the Egyptian god Serapis but now known to have been one of the empire's largest markets. Puteoli was the main imperial port and retained its importance even after the Port of Ostia was upgraded by Emperor Trajan in the 2nd century.

Archaeological site at Pozzuoli

⑤ Baia
MAP B3 ■ 800 60 06 01 or
081 193 057 80 ■ Adm

This little town was the most sumptuous resort of the ancient world – everyone who was anyone had a seaside retreat of daunting size and opulent luxury. Due to the seismic activity in this area, however, much of the land and the structures are now underwater, forming a unique flooded city that can be explored by dives or by boat (see p63). There's also a 15th-century castle here, the Castello di Baia, housing an archaeological museum, while to the north is Lago d'Averno, a crater lake that the ancients believed marked the entrance to the Underworld.

Underwater city, Baia

THE BURNING FIELDS

Flegrei and Phlegrean derive from a Greek word *phlegraios* (burning), applied in ancient times to this zone of perpetual, low-level volcanic activity. **(below)** Below the earth's surface here, magma (molten rock) is flowing, applying pressure upward, making it one of the most unstable regions of the earth's crust, literally littered with volcanic cones and craters.

Anfiteatro Flavio

⑥ Anfiteatro Flavio
MAP C3 ■ Corso Terracciano 75
■ 081 526 60 07 ■ Open 9am–2pm
Wed–Mon (to 7pm summer) ■ Adm

This is the third-largest Roman amphitheatre in the world, after those at Rome and Capua – again making it clear how important this area was to the empire. It seated 40,000 and was equipped with an array of below-floor apparatus for making the *venationes* (wild animal "hunts") that took place as theatrical as possible. Nowhere are such systems so well preserved, due to the lower portion of the structure having been buried until modern times.

⑦ Capo Posillipo
MAP J2

The ancient Greeks called the area Pausilypon ("respite from pain") due to the great beauty of the place. Through the ages, it retained its appeal due to a succession of inhabitants and visitors, from religious communities in medieval times to holiday resorts for the Spanish aristocracy in the 17th century. The Spartan years of the 1950s, however, put an end to that famous beauty in large swaths with the unregulated spread of ugly apartment buildings. Fortunately, parts of the area down by the water still retain great charm, mainly the 17th-century Villa Volpicelli, appearing like a floating castle at the water's edge.

8 Museo Archeologico dei Campi Flegrei

MAP B3 ▪ Via Castello 15, Bacoli
▪ 081 523 37 97 ▪ Open 9am–3pm
Tue–Sun ▪ Adm

The archaeological museum (inside Castello Aragonese di Baia) contains a reassembled *sacellum* (shrine) featuring statues of several emperors. There's also a reconstruction of a *nymphaeum* (fountain), the original of which lies under 6 m (20 ft) of water. Its statues have been raised and tell the story of how Ulysses escaped from the Cyclops Polyphemus.

9 Cumae

MAP B3 ▪ Via Montecuma
▪ Open 9am–7pm daily ▪ Adm

Founded in the 8th century BC, Cumae played a big part in history, due to its seeress. The Cumaean Sibyl, priestess of Apollo, was an oracle who exerted great influence, and the leaders of Rome depended on her prophecies in times of crisis. Sibyl's Grotto, with its weird trapezoidal entrance tunnel, is an enigmatic experience (see p63).

Italian gardens, Reggia di Caserta

10 Reggia di Caserta

MAP D1 ▪ Via Douhet 22 ▪ 0823 44 80 84 ▪ Palace apartments: open 8:30am–7:30pm Wed–Mon; park: open 8:30am–2 hours before sunset Wed–Mon ▪ Adm ▪ www.reggiadi caserta.beniculturali.it

Neapolitan Baroque at its most refined, this 18th-century palace is set around four courtyards with lavish rooms, highlighted by the Great Staircase and the Throne Room. The park has huge decorated fountains, culminating in the Grande Cascata.

A MORNING IN ANCIENT POZZUOLI

▶ Start the tour in the cool of the morning with a visit to **Solfatara** (see p114), the vast volcanic lava cap about 1 km (0.5 mile) north of the town. This stark, bizarre site will set the tone for the day's musings on the ephemeral nature of all things. Next, head back towards town on the **Via Vecchia di San Gennaro** and take a quick left on **Via Domiziana**, which follows the ancient Roman road of basalt stones built to link Rome to Puteoli (Pozzuoli; see p111). Visit the **Santuario di San Gennaro** (see p114) and see the spot where Naples' patron saint met his martyrdom under Emperor Diocletian.

From here, turn back and go down Via Vecchia di San Gennaro to the **Piscina Cardito**, a 2nd-century cistern with a vaulted ceiling supported by pillars. Continue on to the great **Anfiteatro Flavio** and try to imagine what it might have been like, with full scenery and exotic beasts springing out of trapdoors. Next, follow Via Terracciano along to the **Terme di Nettuno**, huge terraced baths, and on the opposite slope the Ninfeo di Diana, a fountain that may have been part of the baths.

Work your way down towards the ancient port, most of it now underwater, to the Serapeum (market). Then walk up onto the promontory, the **Rione Terra**, to explore the 2,000-year-old **Duomo** (cathedral).

Finally, enjoy a well-deserved lunch at the **Antica Trattoria da Ciuffiello** (see p115).

See map on pp110–11 ←

The Best of the Rest

1 Science City, Bagnoli
MAP J2 ▪ Via Coroglio 104
▪ 081 735 22 20/22 ▪ Open 9:30am–2pm Tue–Sat; 10am–7pm Sun ▪ Adm
This hands-on science centre is designed to educate and amuse kids of all ages *(see p64)*.

2 Santa Maria del Faro, Posillipo
MAP J2 ▪ Via Marechiaro 96a ▪ 081 769 14 39 ▪ Open during services
Dating back to the 1300s, this church was probably built over the remains of a Roman *faro* (lighthouse). It was restored in the 18th century.

3 War Memorial Mausoleo, Posillipo
MAP J2 ▪ Via Belsito
▪ Open 7am–noon Tue–Sun
This altar is dedicated to the lost lives of World War I. The astonishing structure shows caryatids gazing as if possessed by grief.

4 Astroni
MAP C3 ▪ Riserva degli Astroni, Agnano ▪ 081 588 37 20 ▪ Open 9:30am–2pm daily ▪ Adm
The Romans tapped the geothermal properties of this volcanic crater to build their spas.

5 Solfatara, Pozzuoli
MAP C3 ▪ Via Solfatara 161
▪ 081 526 23 41/74 13 ▪ Open 8:30am–6pm daily ▪ Adm ▪ www.solfatara.it
Above the town, a crater of a dormant volcano presents an unearthly landscape. The Romans called it *Forum Vulcani* (Vulcan's Forum).

Volcanic landscape at Solfatara

6 Palazzo Donn'Anna, Posillipo
MAP J2 ▪ Piazza Donn'Anna 9
▪ Closed to the public
The air of mystery that envelops this 17th-century palace has given rise to rumours. One claims Queen Joan II used it for illicit trysts, after which she had her lovers tossed into the sea.

7 Benevento
MAP F1
This town's pride and joy is the well-preserved Arch of Trajan, chronicling the Roman emperor's civic works.

Arch of Trajan, Benevento

8 Santuario di San Gennaro, Pozzuoli
MAP C3 ▪ Via S Gennaro Agnano 10
▪ 081 526 11 14 ▪ Open 8am–noon, 4:30–8pm Mon–Sat, 8am–1pm, 4:30–8pm Sun
This 16th-century church is said to mark the spot where Naples' patron saint was decapitated, and the brown stain on a stone is said to be his blood.

9 Bacoli
MAP B4 ▪ Via A Greco 10 ▪ Open 9am–1 hour before sunset daily
Noteworthy here is the *Piscina Mirabile*, a cistern used to collect water for the old port of Misenum.

10 Santa Maria Capuavetere
MAP C1
The Appian Way, the first Roman highway, led south to Capua, the "biggest and richest city in Italy", according to Livy in the 1st century BC.

Places to Eat

PRICE CATEGORIES
For a three-course meal for one with half a bottle of wine (or equivalent meal), taxes and extra charges.

€ under €30 €€ €30–€50 €€€ over €50

1 Gelateria Bilancione, Posillipo

MAP J2 ▪ Via Posillipo 238B

Choose your favourite *gelato* at this ice cream shop and then enjoy it sitting on a bench taking in the vista.

2 Giuseppone a Mare, Posillipo

MAP J2 ▪ Via Russo 13 ▪ 081 19 13 77 03 ▪ Closed Mon, Sun L ▪ €€

Renowned since 1889, the seafood is excellent. Popular for receptions and celebrations, so book ahead.

3 Antica Trattoria da Ciuffiello, Pozzuoli

MAP C3 ▪ Via Dicearchia 11 bis ▪ 081 526 93 97 ▪ Closed Mon (winter) ▪ €€

Overlooking the central piazza, this restaurant is well known for its grilled specialities. Their consummate *zuppa di pesce* (fish soup) is a meal all in itself.

4 Il Casolare da Tobia, Bacoli

MAP B4 ▪ Via Fabris 12 ▪ 081 523 51 93 ▪ €

Wonderful organically grown food, from the rich volcanic soil of the crater on which the place is perched. It is best to book ahead.

5 La Ninfea, Pozzuoli

MAP C3 ▪ Via C Colombo 21 ▪ 081 853 13 37 ▪ No credit cards ▪ €€

A speciality here is *schiaffoni alla ninfea*, a delicious seafood pasta dish.

6 Vinaria, Pozzuoli

MAP C3 ▪ Via Monte di Cuma 3 ▪ 081 804 62 35 ▪ Closed Mon–Thu ▪ €€€

This restaurant boasts its own piece of history with Roman ruins discovered on site. The wine list highlights bottles from Camania and those produced in the Campi Flegrei.

7 Leucio, Casertavecchia-San Leucio

MAP D1 ▪ Strada Panoramica ▪ 082 330 12 41 ▪ Closed Mon, Sun D, 2 wks Aug ▪ €

Take a 10-minute drive north of Caserta to try *risotto vergine*, with squid, prawns and cuttlefish.

8 Féfé, Bacoli

MAP B4 ▪ Via della Shoah 15, Case Vecchie ▪ 081 523 30 11 ▪ Closed Mon D (winter) ▪ €

Filled with regulars, this place faces the port. You are welcomed with the house aperitif and advised of the seafood specials of the day.

9 Al Faro, Posillipo

MAP J2 ▪ Porticciolo de Marechiaro ▪ 081 575 51 42 ▪ Closed Mon, 1 wk Aug ▪ €€

This seafood restaurant is known for its romantic atmosphere and wonderful views. The catches of the day are served up in sumptuous style.

Spaghetti alle vongole veraci, Al Faro

10 Da Gino e Pina, Benevento

MAP F1 ▪ Viale dell' Università 1 ▪ 082 42 49 47 ▪ Closed Sun, Aug ▪ €

A popular family-run restaurant serving traditional cuisine using local produce. Try the homemade pasta in local saffron liqueur. Good desserts.

See map on pp110–11

Streetsmart

**Elegant shopping arcades of
Galleria Umberto I, Naples**

Getting To and Around Naples and the Amalfi Coast

Arriving by Air

The **Capodichino Airport** in Naples is 5.9 km (3.7 miles) northeast of the city centre. National and international flights arrive from all the main Italian cities and most major European ones.

Alitalia is the main carrier within Italy. Major European airlines offer connections to Naples, including **British Airways**, **Air France**, **Lufthansa** and **Iberia**, as well as low-cost carriers like **easyJet**.

Taxis are located outside the arrivals hall, as well as several car rental companies. The regular **Alibus** service runs from the airport to Napoli Centrale train station and Piazza Municipio, giving access to the Naples Molo Beverello for a ferry to Sorrento and the islands. **Curreri Viaggi** also offer a bus service from the airport to Sorrento.

Arriving by Train

The train service to Naples is operated by Italy's national rail company, **Trenitalia**, and by **Italo**. Naples' main station is called Centrale, which offers connections to local bus and Metro lines, as well as the **Circumvesuviana** train.

Keep in mind that there are no train stations on the Amalfi Coast. The closest is in Salerno, which is serviced by both Trenitalia and Italo. Another option is to take the Circumvesuviana train

to Sorrento. From both Salerno and Sorrento there are buses and ferries to various places on the Amalfi Coast.

Arriving by Sea

A very pleasant way of travelling to this part of Italy is by boat. Ferry and hydrofoil services run from Sardinia, Sicily, the Aeolian Islands and many other Mediterranean ports. Cruise ships also make stops in Naples and along the coast.

Arriving by Road

Reaching Naples by car is possible but it is by no means advisable for the uninitiated. As you hit Naples, there are so many perplexing inter-changes, with inadequate signage, that it is easy to get lost. Driving along the twisty and narrow Amalfi Coast road is also an adventure. Given the intense driving experience and extremely challenging parking, many travellers prefer to arrive and travel around Naples or the Amalfi Coast by other methods of transport.

Arriving by Bus

The regular bus and coach services are a good way to get to Naples and other towns in the area. If arriving by bus in Naples you will find yourself in one of the main squares, Piazza Garibaldi, in front of the Centrale train station.

Getting Around by Train and Metro

Naples and its vicinity has a complex but reliable transport system (**ANM**), including trams, funicular railways and light railways that serve outlying areas. There is also a Metro system in Naples and most lines converge at the Centrale train station.

The Circumvesuviana train goes to Sorrento, with stops along the way, including archaeological sites such as Pompeii. The Cumana and Circumflegreo trains go west to the Campi Flegrei.

By Bus

The city buses in Naples are not for the faint-hearted. The system is chaotic and the old buses are dirty, crowded and subject to traffic jams. Most bus lines have their terminus at Piazza Garibaldi. Buy tickets from any local bar before boarding and validate them once on board. Open-top, hop-on hop-off **City Sightseeing** buses depart from Piazza Municipio and are a fun way to discover Naples, as well as Sorrento and the Amalfi Coast. The Amalfi Coast is also served by the **SITA** bus company.

By Boat

Once here, you could stick to ferries, going from port to port (though ferries do not run on the

Amalfi Coast from November to March/April). Naples has two ports, then there are the islands, Amalfi, Pozzuoli, Sorrento, Positano and Salerno. Companies include **Alilauro**, **Caremar**, **SNAV** and **Travelmar**.

Tickets

Unico Campania offers 1-day or weekly tickets for integrated travel in Naples and regional areas in Campania. For the Amalfi Coast, look for the **Unico Costiera** tickets that can be purchased per route or 1- or 3-day passes. Validate tickets before departure by stamping them in the machine on board.

By Taxi

There are taxi ranks throughout Naples and at the airport. Set fares are in place and a list of tariffs with surcharges must be displayed. A taxi from the airport to the town centre is about €30. Companies include **Consortaxi**, **Consorzio Taxi**, **GESCAB** and **Radio Taxi La Partenope**.

By Car

The minimum age for renting a car is 21, but some companies will charge extra below the age of 25. Most companies require that you be covered for any eventual problem, including collision damage and theft.

Getting around by car in Naples and along the Amalfi Coast area is likely to stress even the calmest of drivers (cars are not allowed on Capri). Traffic jams on the Sorrentine Peninsula and the Amalfi Coast are maddening, car theft is common, the motorways are chaotic and confusing, and parking is impossible.

By Bicycle and Motorcycle

Navigating the chaotic traffic in and around Naples on two wheels is not recommended. It's a better option on the islands of Procida and Ischia, the mountainous backroads along the Sorrentine Peninsula and the Amalfi Coast; but be prepared for narrow roads and surprises around every twist and turn.

On Foot

The sights of central Naples are easy enough to get around on foot. Walking is also a good way to explore villages along the Amalfi Coast, which are made up of staircases and narrow alleys. The area is blessed with mountain trails for hiking. Some of them thread their way along old goat paths from village to village.

DIRECTORY

ARRIVING BY AIR

Air France
w airfrance.com

Alibus
w anm.it

Alitalia
w alitalia.it

British Airways
w britishairways.com

Capodichino Airport
w aeroportodinapoli.it

Curreri Viaggi
w curreriviaggi.it

easyJet
w easyjet.com

Iberia
w iberia.com

Lufthansa
w lufthansa.com

ARRIVING BY TRAIN

Circumvesuviana
w eavsrl.it

Italo
w italotreno.it

Trenitalia
w trenitalia.com

TRAIN, METRO AND BUS

ANM
w anm.it

City Sightseeing
w city-sightseeing.it

SITA
w sitasudtrasporti.it

BOAT

Alilauro
w alilauro.it

Caremar
w caremar.it

SNAV
w snav.it

Travelmar
w travelmar.it

TICKETS

Unico Campania/Costiera
w unicocampania.it

TAXI

Consortaxi
w consortaxi.com

Consorzio Taxi Napoli
w consorziotaxinapoli.it

GESCAB
w gescab.it

Radio Taxi La Partenope
w radiotaxilapartenope.it

Practical Information

Passports and Visas

Citizens of the EU can use their national identity cards to enter Italy. Visitors from outside the EU need a valid passport to enter the country. Travellers from the US, Australia, New Zealand, Canada and Japan do not need a visa for stays of up to three months as long as the passport is valid for six months beyond the date of entry. For longer stays, a visa is necessary and can be obtained at the **Ministry of Foreign Affairs** before arrival, and once in Italy you should apply at the local *questura* (police station) for a *permesso di soggiorno*.

Other nationalities should check entry details at their local embassy or consulate. Italian consulates in your home country can be good sources for detailed information, including tourism, employment, and residency in Italy.

Travel Safety Advice

Visitors can get up-to-date travel safety information from the **Foreign and Commonwealth Office** in the UK, the **State Department** in the US, and the **Department of Foreign Affairs and Trade** in Australia.

Customs Regulations

Italian customs is run by the **Agenzia delle Dogane e dei Monopoli**. Their "Traveller's Customs Charter" gives details of the import and export regulations. There are no limits for EU citizens on most goods carried in or out of Italy as long as they are for personal use. Travellers can import from EU countries: 800 cigarettes, 400 cigarillos, 1kg (2.2 lb) of smoking tobacco, 10 litres of spirits over 22 per cent proof, 20 litres of alcoholic beverages under 22 per cent, 90 litres of wine (no more than 60 litres of sparkling wine) and 110 litres of beer. Travellers from non-EU countries can import 200 cigarettes, 100 cigarillos, 50 cigars, 250 gr of smoking tobacco, 1 litre of spirits over 22 per cent proof, 2 litres of alcoholic beverages under 22 per cent, 4 litres of wine and 16 litres of beer.

Non-EU residents can claim a VAT refund on EU purchases *(see p124)*.

Travel Insurance

All travellers are advised to buy insurance against theft or loss, accidents, illness and travel delays or cancellations. Italy has a reciprocal health agreement with other EU countries, and EU citizens are automatically entitled to medical care in Italy if they have a valid European Health Insurance Card (EHIC). Non-EU visitors should check if their country has reciprocal arrangements with Italy.

Emergency Services

For emergencies, there are dedicated numbers for the **Carabinieri** (police), **State Police**, **Fire Brigade** and **Ambulance**.

Health

Italy does not require any vaccinations, and there are few health hazards. Tap water is potable; however, many Italians prefer to drink bottled water.

For minor ailments, look for the green or red cross sign indicating a *farmacia* (pharmacy). Pharmacists in Italy are highly trained and can serve as surrogate doctors, and they can usually prescribe just the right thing if your symptoms are clear. Often, drugs that would require a prescription in your home country can be sold without one in Italy. If you need to fill a specific prescription, it's important to know the actual chemical in question and not just its brand name, as it may be different in Italy. Pharmacies keep regular shop hours, but there will always be at least one in the area that is open outside normal hours. Look for the list posted next to the door of any *farmacia*, which will show the schedule of off-hour openings nearby.

There are hospitals *(see Directory)* covering most of the Amalfi Coast that provide 24-hour emergency care. If you would prefer an English-speaking doctor, contact your country's consulate in Naples for recommended doctors.

Personal Security

Naples' reputation as an unsafe city has improved drastically. However, like any large city it is best to be cautious. Leave all valuables, including your passport, in a hotel safety deposit box. Pickpockets are not uncommon in crowded parts of Naples, particularly on public transport. Keep your valuables tucked away in unreachable places. Carry wallets in front pockets and ensure bags are strapped across your front. In restaurants and cafés, keep your personal belongings on your lap or tied to your person. Losses or thefts should be reported to the nearest police station.

Though petty thievery is part of the scene in Naples, violent crimes are quite rare. Such things generally occur only in the underworld of organized crime far from the regular tourist spots.

Compared to Northern Europe, attitudes towards women travellers can be quite macho in the Naples area. Still, women generally do not encounter excessive harassment and can travel alone without a problem, especially on the Sorrentine Peninsula and the islands. Naturally, it is best for women to exercise normal care, especially after dark. Women shouldn't stay around Naples' central train station if travelling on their own.

Travellers with Disabilities

Getting around in a wheelchair in Naples and the Amalfi Coast area is a near impossibility without assistance. The larger museums and sights are making some headway at providing easier access. Although progress is slow, things are improving gradually, as more and more places try to upgrade in order to conform to EU standards. Disabled visitors will, without a doubt, require help from travelling companions at every stage of their journey.

Many older buildings, which are normally refurbished medieval structures, are often without facilities for wheelchair users – there are endless stairways and levels to contend with, sometimes even within a single room. The only reliable option is to stay in the newest hotel you can find, where lifts will probably be big enough and bathroom sizes will all comply with EU laws. Double-check the facilities on offer before booking anything.

DIRECTORY

PASSPORTS AND VISAS

Ministry of Foreign Affairs
W vistoperitalia.esteri.it

US Consulate
MAP J6 ■ Piazza della Repubblica
W naples.usconsulate.gov

TRAVEL SAFETY ADVICE

Australia Department of Foreign Affairs and Trade
W dfat.gov.au
W smartraveller.gov.au

UK Foreign and Commonwealth Office
W gov.uk/foreign-travel-advice

US State Department
W travel.state.gov

CUSTOMS

Agenzia delle Dogane e dei Monopoli
W agenziadogane monopoli.gov.it

EMERGENCY SERVICES

Ambulance
C 118

Carabinieri
C 112

Fire Brigade
C 115

State Police
C 113

HOSPITALS

Amalfi Coast
Via Civita, Castiglione di Ravello
C 089 871 122

Capri
MAP T2 ■ Via Provinciale Anacapri 3, Capri
C 081 838 12 27

Ischia
Anna Rizzoli
Via Fundera 2, Lacco Ameno
C 081 507 91 11

Naples
Ospedale Cardarelli
Via Cardarelli 9
C 081 747 11 11

Sorrento
Civico
Corso Italia 1
C 081 533 11 11

Currency and Banking

Italy uses the euro (€), which is divided into 100 cents. Paper notes are in denominations of €500, €200, €100, €50, €20, €10 and €5. Coins are €2, €1, 50c, 20c, 10c, 5c, 2c and 1c.

ATMs (called *bancomats* in Italy) are the easiest and safest way to get cash while travelling and are also a good way to beat commission charges at *bureaux de change*. Italian ATMs charge no transaction fee; you'll only have your own bank's fee to pay for using a non-branch machine and possibly a foreign transaction fee. If you withdraw the maximum each time (usually €300) the fee will likely be only about 1 per cent. Banks also normally offer better exchange and commission rates than *bureaux de change* or hotels, although rates can vary from bank to bank.

Credit cards are widely accepted in most large places. Only restaurants and smaller businesses may find it a problem, because of the 2–4 per cent commission that card companies charge them. Be aware that your own bank may charge you a 2 per cent currency conversion fee for every card purchase you make. If your credit card is lost or stolen, inform the local police and your credit card company immediately.

Telephone and Internet

The dialling code for Italy is 39, and when calling any number in Italy you must include the area code that starts with a zero. To call outside Italy, dial 00 then the country code, area code and number.

Most mobile phones will work in Italy, but it is advisable to check with your provider before departure. Consider buying a local SIM card to avoid high roaming charges. SIM cards are inexpensive and readily available from Italy's largest cell phone providers: TIM, Wind, Vodafone and Tre.

Free Wi-Fi is available at many hotels, cafés and restaurants. However, smaller hotels may still charge for internet or only provide it in the lobby.

Postal Services

Main branches of Italy's **Poste Italiane** post offices are open 8:30am–7pm Monday to Friday and 8:30am–noon on Saturdays. In smaller branches, rural towns or villages the post offices will often be open only 8:30am–1pm from Monday to Saturday. Mailboxes are red and have two slots – one *"per la città"* (local) and one *"per tutte le altre destinazioni"* (everywhere else).

Stamps (*francobolli*) are on sale at post offices and tobacconists (*tabacchi*), and often (unofficially) at any shop selling postcards.

TV, Radio and Newspapers

Most hotels will have satellite TV and the international news channels that come with it. Many programs on Sky satellite TV channels can be switched to the original language. The popular local radio station in the Naples area is **Radio Kiss Kiss** (95.9FM).

Newsstands and book-shops sell a selection of Italian and international press. *USA Today* and the *International Herald Tribune* are generally available in tourist areas, along with most major British, German and French newspapers. The local newspaper published in Naples is *Il Mattino*, while the online newspaper **The Local** covers Italian news in English. For events in and around Naples, pick up a copy of the free monthly magazine *Qui Napoli*.

Opening Hours

Post office hours are generally 9am–6pm Monday to Friday, although during August many businesses close mid-afternoon or entirely.

Shops are usually open from 9am–2pm and 4–8pm, except in popular tourist areas where they will likely remain open through the lunch *riposo*.

Many shops, hotels and restaurants close for part or all of the holiday season, especially on the Amalfi Coast, Capri and Ischia. Banks generally open 8:30am–1:30pm and 3–4pm from Monday to Friday.

Museums and galleries have their own opening hours, which may change with the season, especially in coastal areas and the islands. Museums and historic sites will often close one day per week, even in high season. It is best to check their websites before you visit.

Nearly all banks, shops and businesses are closed on public holidays: New Year's Day, Epiphany (6 Jan), Easter, Easter Monday, Liberation Day (25 Apr), Labour Day (1 May), Republic Day (2 Jun), Ferragosto (15 Aug), All Saints Day (1 Nov), Immaculate Conception (8 Dec), Christmas Day (25 Dec) and the Feast of St Stephen (26 Dec).

Time Difference

Italy is one hour ahead of Greenwich Mean Time (GMT) and 6 hours ahead of US Eastern Standard Time (EST). The clock moves forward 1 hour for daylight saving time from the last Sunday in March until the last Sunday in October.

Electrical Appliances

Italy uses plugs with two or three round pins and an electrical voltage and frequency of 220V/50Hz. Devices from other countries will require adapters and may need voltage converters.

Visitor Information

Naples has two main **Azienda Autonoma di Soggiorno** (ASST) offices in the historic centre, one near Galleria Umberto I and the other at Piazza del Gesù. Free maps, brochures and information on events and attractions are available here in multiple languages. You can also contact the Italian Tourist Board in your home country for such information before your departure.

Along the Amalfi Coast, tourist information offices are located in Amalfi, Positano and Ravello. Sorrento and the islands of Capri and Ischia also have official information offices.

A number of websites can help you research exactly which parts and how much of the fascinating area you want to cover during your visit. A notable example is the **Napoli Unplugged** website, which has detailed information in English on transport, history, events and things to see and do in Naples.

Useful apps include Google Maps, Google Translate, TripAdvisor for restaurant reviews, and **Travelmar** for purchasing tickets for ferries along the Amalfi Coast, all available for Android and iOS devices.

DIRECTORY

POSTAL SERVICES

Poste Italiane
w posteitaliane.it

TV, RADIO AND NEWSPAPERS

Il Mattino
w ilmattino.it

The Local
w thelocal.it

Qui Napoli
w inaples.it/ita/quinapoli.htm

Radio Kiss Kiss
w kisskiss.it

VISITOR INFORMATION

Azienda Autonoma di Soggiorno Cura e Turismo Amalfi
Via delle Repubbliche Marinare
c 089 87 11 07

w amalfitouristoffice.it

Azienda Autonoma di Soggiorno Cura e Turismo Ischia and Procida
Via Sogliuzzo 72, Ischia
c 081 507 42 11
w infoischiaprocida.it

Azienda Autonoma di Soggiorno Cura e Turismo Isola di Capri
Piazza Cerio Ignazio 11
c 081 837 53 08
w capritourism.com

Azienda Autonoma di Soggiorno Cura e Turismo Napoli
MAP N5 ■ Via San Carlo 9
c 081 40 23 94
MAP N3 ■ Piazza del Gesù
c 081 551 27 01
w inaples.it

Azienda Autonoma di Soggiorno Cura e Turismo Positano
Via Regina Giovanna 3
c 089 87 50 67
w aziendaturismo positano.it

Azienda Autonoma di Soggiorno Cura e Turismo Ravello
Via Roma 18
c 089 85 70 96
w ravellotime.com

Azienda Autonoma di Soggiorno Cura e Turismo Sorrento
Via Luigi De Maio 35
c 081 807 40 33
w sorrentotourism.com

Napoli Unplugged
w napoliunplugged.com

Travelmar
w www.travelmar.it

Weather

The climate is typically Mediterranean, with warm summers and cool winters. July and August are very hot and humid, with temperatures around 30°–40° C (85°–105° F). The best weather is generally found in spring and autumn. March, April and September tend to be the rainiest months. Winter is cold, dark and rainy, but can offer dramatic views of Vesuvius's peak dusted with snow.

For culture, visit Naples in the winter, when you'll get a real feel for local life and fewer crowds at the popular sites. For swimming, it's difficult to avoid the hot months but to side-step the crowds, June or September are a better bet than July and August, which is when most of Italy will be on holiday with you. To appreciate the beauty of the natural setting and the quality of life, any time of year is ideal. Most hotels and restaurants on the Amalfi Coast and islands close for a period or the entire winter.

Trips and Tours

With a wealth of history and culture, there are many different ways to enjoy a visit Naples. Walking is one of the best ways to explore the city, especially in the historic centre. Get a good introduction to Naples on a walking tour by **Free Walking Tour Napoli**.

A visit to Naples isn't complete without delving deeper into the local cuisine. From making your own Neapolitan pizza to sampling the best sweets, **Eat in Italy** provide cooking lessons and food tours led by experienced locals.

For a more in-depth look at Naples' rich archaeological sites, world-class museums and distinctive culture, **Context Travel** offers unique and highly informative tours led by local historians and academics.

You will see another side of Naples by going underground with **Napoli Sotterranea**. Tours lead far underground and back through history, from Greek-Roman aqueducts to areas used as shelters during World War II.

For local tours in Naples and guided excursions to Pompeii, Capri, Sorrento and the Amalfi Coast, try the family-run company **Rimonti Tours**.

In summer, there is no better way to see the coastline than by boat. Local family-run company **Gennaro e Salvatore** operate personalized tours to admire the beautiful caves and bays, stopping to take a dip here and there.

Shopping

Naples is an excellent shopping destination, with all the big Italian brands represented as well as a large selection of boutiques for designer fashion, accessories and home decor. For upmarket shopping, the Chiaia neighbourhood has the finest selection of designer boutiques. Men's fashion is especially refined in Naples. For more popular brand name shopping, Via Toledo, Galleria Umberto I (see p88) and the historic centre are the best bet.

While exploring the Sorrento Peninsula and islands, great buys include locally made ceramics, handmade paper in Amalfi, hand-carved cameos or handmade leather sandals. You'll also find local wines, cheeses, and the popular *limoncello* liqueur. Check for any restrictions on importing foodstuffs into your home country before you buy.

There are two main sales periods per year that are determined by the Italian government for each region. Summer sales usually start at the beginning of July and run for 60 days. Winter sales begin around Epiphany (6 Jan) and run until March.

Prices include VAT (IVA in Italian), which currently stands at 22 per cent on most purchases. For non-EU residents, VAT refunds are available for purchases over €155 that will be taken outside the EU. You will need to ask the sales clerk for a form or card at the time of purchase (note that not all shops participate in VAT returns). VAT can be redeemed at the customs counter in the airport at your last point of departure from the EU.

Where to Eat

Famous as the birthplace of pizza and many Italian favourites, Neapolitan cuisine is loved around the world. Restaurants in Naples and the surrounding area are primarily dedicated to Neapolitan cooking, and international cuisine options are hard to find. Yet with such a delightful variety of options, from seafood to delicious meat recipes, it's rarely a problem to find something for every taste. With an endless variety of traditional Neapolitan vegetable recipes, there is never a shortage of choices on the menu for vegetarians and vegans.

Restaurants usually open from 1–3pm for lunch and 7–10:30pm for dinner. Italians generally eat dinner from 8–9:30pm, so expect to find the best atmosphere around that time. In popular tourist areas some restaurants may serve continuously. Cafés are often open for light meals throughout the day.

Restaurants rarely have children's menus available, but are usually happy to prepare special pasta dishes for customers. Few restaurants have high chairs, or perhaps just one or two for the entire establishment.

Where to Stay

There is something for all tastes and budgets in the Naples and Amalfi Coast area, whether you're looking for five-star luxury, a charming villa rental in a secluded spot or a budget-friendly hostel. In Naples, the most convenient places to stay are in the centre of the city, making them accessible to all the main sights. Naples is also a good base for exploring

Pompeii, Vesuvius and the islands *(see pp131–2)*.

The Amalfi Coast and Capri have long held a reputation for being expensive, with many luxurious hotels having taken advantage of the spectacular landscape. You will get what you pay for, however, as service and facilities are of a very high standard. Cheaper alternatives can be found in smaller towns, such as Praiano, but even Positano and Ravello offer some budget accommodation *(see pp130–31)*.

Sorrento's reputation as a luxury resort is well founded, although there is no shortage of cheaper hotels – you will just find yourself further from the centre of things and with less breathtaking views *(see pp129–30)*.

Rates are the highest during peak season in the summer and during Easter and Christmas. Booking well in advance is recommended for the period from Easter through to October, especially for the Amalfi Coast, Capri and Sorrento. Low season specials are abundant in Naples and shoulder season bargains are sometimes available along the coastal areas and islands. Contrary to the high season rates and crowds in the Amalfi Coast, August can be quieter in Naples with some hotels offering lower tariffs.

Most hotels and hostels now have online booking or subscribe to major booking websites. **Airbnb**, **Booking.com** and **Hotels.com** have extensive listings for

Naples and the surrounding areas. It is always worth checking prices at the establishment itself as they often feature offers that are not available on booking websites. **Hostels of Naples** provides information about the best hostels in Naples, Capri, Ischia, Sorrento and the Amalfi Coast. **Summer in Italy** specializes in holiday villa rentals in Capri, Sorrento and on the Amalfi Coast. If you are looking to stay with private families, **Rent a Bed** offers a range of choices and areas in Naples and on the coast.

DIRECTORY

TRIPS AND TOURS

Context Travel
w contexttravel.com

Eat in Italy
w eatinitaly
foodtours.com

**Free Walking
Tour Napoli**
w freewalking
tournapoli.com

Gennaro e Salvatore
w gennaroesalvatore.it

Napoli Sotterranea
w napolisotterranea.org

Rimonti Tours
w rimontitours.com

WHERE TO STAY

Airbnb
w airbnb.com

Booking.com
w booking.com

Hostels of Naples
w hostelsofnaples.com

Hotels.com
w hotels.com

Rent a Bed
w rentabed.it

Summer in Italy
w summerinitaly.com

Places to Stay

Luxury Hotels in Naples

Costantinopoli 104
MAP N2 ■ Via S Maria di Costantinopoli 104 ■ 081 557 10 35 ■ www.costan tinopoli104.it ■ DA ■ €€
This stylish hotel, with stained-glass windows and wrought-iron work, is housed in an Art Nouveau villa. Some rooms have a terrace. There is a pool too.

Hotel San Francesco al Monte
MAP K2 ■ Corso Vittorio Emanuele 328, Vomero ■ 081 423 91 11 ■ www. sanfrancescoalmonte.it ■ DA ■ €€
A former 16th-century Franciscan monastery where the now-luxurious former monks' cells have views over the bay, and there's a garden restaurant with more vistas.

Hotel Una
MAP R2 ■ Piazza Garibaldi 9/10 ■ 081 563 69 01 ■ www.unahotels.it ■ DA ■ €€
Part of a Florentine hotel chain, this restored 19th-century palazzo has a luxury interior with spacious rooms. The rooftop bar has great views.

Miramare
MAP N6 ■ Via Nazario Sauro 24 ■ 081 764 75 89 ■ www.hotelmiramare. com ■ €€
Built in 1914 as an aristocratic villa, this modernized hotel has retained its original Art Nouveau style. Located right on the bay, its lovely terrace and many rooms afford spectacular views.

Palazzo Caracciolo
MAP Q1 ■ Via Carbonara 112 ■ 081 016 01 11 ■ www.accorhotels.com ■ DA ■ €€
This regal hotel was once the home of the aristocratic Caracciolo family, where famous guests such as the king of Naples and Napoleon's brother-in-law were welcomed. Near the Duomo, enjoy elegant surroundings and modern comfort in this intimate, upmarket hotel.

Paradiso
MAP J2 ■ Via Catullo 11 ■ 081 247 51 11 ■ www. hotelparadisonapoli.it ■ €€
A Best Western chain hotel but Mediterranean in feel. Perched on Posillipo Hill, it's far from the city chaos and has a terrace restaurant with a stunning view of Vesuvius.

Grand Hotel Parker's
MAP L4 ■ Corso Vittorio Emanuele 135 ■ 081 761 24 74 ■ www.grandhotel parkers.it ■ DA ■ €€€
This fine old hotel was a Grand Tour stopover. Restored to its former glory, it boasts antiques, chandeliers and original art. Be sure to visit the wonderful library, full of antiquarian books. There are two restaurants, one with postcard views from the roof garden, and an in-house spa.

Grand Hotel Santa Lucia
Via Partenope 46 ■ 081 764 06 66 ■ www. santalucia.it ■ DA ■ €€€
Though more modest, this hotel has the most character of the three "grands" that stand along the bay. It has views of the Castel dell'Ovo and has a tasteful Art Nouveau decor, along with all the comforts you may require.

Grand Hotel Vesuvio
Via Partenope 45 ■ 081 764 00 44 ■ www. vesuvio.it ■ DA ■ €€€
A 1950s reincarnation of the original 1882 grandeur, which was obliterated during World War II. It is consequently lacking in some of the charm of its neighbours, but is still the preferred lodging of many visiting VIPs. It is very well positioned, and the sea views from the upper floors are terrific.

Hotel Excelsior
Via Partenope 48 ■ 081 764 01 11 ■ www.euro starsexcelsior.com ■ €€€
This belle époque palazzo is the grande dame of Naples' plush hotels, and it has seen everyone from movie royalty to monarchs pass through its elegant doors. Another of the waterfront hotels, Excelsior has commanding views of the entire bay, Vesuvius and Castel dell'Ovo.

Good-Value Hotels in Naples

Hotel 241 Correra
MAP N2 ▪ Via Carrera 241 ▪ 081 19 56 28 42 ▪ www. correra.it ▪ DA ▪ €
Close to the Museo Archeologico Nazionale, this little oasis is reached through a gate leading to a discreet doorway. Beyond is a colourful hotel with sunny terrace and large, bright, airy rooms. Good breakfasts.

Mercure Napoli Angioino Centro
MAP N4 ▪ Via A Depretis 123 ▪ 081 552 95 00 ▪ www.accorhotels.com ▪ DA ▪ €
Part of an international chain and very modern, this is a comfortable choice in Royal Naples.

Neapolis
MAP N2 ▪ Via Francesco del Giudice 13 ▪ 081 442 08 15 ▪ www.leterrazzedi neapolis.com ▪ DA ▪ €
Up-to-the-minute services include a computer in your room with internet. The location is handy for the old centre. The decor, though rather Spartan, is comfortable. Frequent special offers are available on their website.

Parteno
MAP L6 ▪ Lungomare Partenope 1 ▪ 081 245 20 95 ▪ €
This establishment insists on calling itself a "bed and breakfast", but it more closely resembles an elegant boutique hotel. The rooms are beautiful, bright and airy and the service most refined. Parteno also offers fully equipped self-catering apartments.

Pinto-Storey
MAP K5 ▪ Via G Martucci 72 ▪ 081 68 12 60 ▪ www. pintostorey.it ▪ €
Dating from 1878 and redolent of bygone days, this hotel is very stylish, with Art Nouveau touches and an overall aura of gentility. It's in one of the nicest parts of town, close to the Villa Comunale. Many rooms have great views of the bay, and air conditioning is available at an extra charge.

Rex
MAP N6 ▪ Via Palepoli 12 ▪ 081 764 93 89 ▪ www. lifestylehotel.it/rex ▪ €
Located by the sea in the Santa Lucia district, around the corner from Naples' bastions of luxury, this hotel is full of period style. Most of the rooms have views and charming balconies. The decor is simple but comfortable, and breakfast is included, served in your room.

Toledo
MAP M4 ▪ Via Montecalvario 15 ▪ 081 40 68 00 ▪ www. hoteltoledo.com ▪ €
Located in a restructured 17th-century palazzo, which is in the earthy Spanish Quarter, the Toledo hotel is situated halfway between Royal Naples and the historic centre. It's convenient for every important monument and for all forms of public transport.

Caravaggio
MAP P2 ▪ Piazza Cardinale Sisto Riario Sforza 157 ▪ 081 211 00 66 ▪ www.caravaggio hotel.it ▪ €€
Housed in a beautifully restored medieval building, in one of the most evocative parts of the old centre, this hotel exudes style. It's right behind the cathedral.

Chiaia Hotel de Charme
MAP M5 ▪ Via Chiaia 216 ▪ 081 41 55 55 ▪ www. chiaiahotel.com ▪ DA ▪ €€
This very special place actually consists of rooms in the restored palace of a Neapolitan marchese. It's appropriately located in Royal Naples so that you can indulge all of your aristocratic fantasies. The rooms are full of original furnishings and each is named after one of your host's noble ancestors.

Hotel Canada
MAP K2 ▪ Via Mergellina 43 ▪ www.seahotels.com ▪ €€
If you want to be in stylish Mergellina with easy access to all the fun of the seafront social life, as well as hydrofoils to the islands, this is the choice. Rooms are homely, with caring touches here and there such as antiques and fresh flowers.

Budget Hotels in Naples

Albergo Duomo
MAP Q3 ▪ Via Duomo 228 ▪ 081 26 59 88 ▪ www. hotelduomonapoli.it ▪ €
Perfectly located for visiting the old centre, this is a basic place, but very well maintained and not without a certain charm. In this price range, you can't do better. Right across the street from the Duomo and just steps away from all the major sights of ancient Naples.

Bella Capri
MAP P4 ▪ Via G Melisurgo 4 ▪ 081 552 94 94 ▪ www. bellacapri.it ▪ €
Located on the main port, with nicely furnished rooms on the sixth floor of a modern block – some have great views of Mount Vesuvius and Capri from the balcony. There are good restaurants in the area.

Europeo
MAP P3 ▪ Via Mezzocannone 109 ▪ 081 551 72 54 ▪ www. hoteleuropeonapoli.com ▪ €
Modern and basic, this hotel is well placed for checking out the university area and the ancient centre. The rooms have a sense of style and some are decorated with wall frescoes. These rooms include breakfast, served on the roof terrace of the nearby Executive Hotel.

Hostel of the Sun
MAP N4 ▪ Via G Melisurgo 15 ▪ 081 420 63 93 ▪ www.hostelnapoli.com ▪ No air conditioning ▪ €
This lively hostel has well-priced dormitories and private rooms, some of which have en-suite bathrooms. The location is excellent; situated near the water, it is a stone's throw from Royal Naples and very convenient for the old centre. The atmosphere is friendly and the staff multilingual.

Hostel-Pensione Mancini
MAP Q2 ▪ Via P S Mancini 33 ▪ 081 553 67 31 ▪ www.hostelpensione mancini.com ▪ €
Located just a 5-minute walk from Centrale train station, this recently refurbished hostel offers both private rooms and dorms. Free Wi-Fi and a communal kitchen, too.

Hotel des Artistes and Hostel
MAP P1 ▪ Via Duomo 61 ▪ 081 192 550 86 ▪ www. hoteldesartistesnaples.it ▪ €
A friendly little place, just a few blocks from the Museo Archeologico in one direction and the Duomo in the other. Set in a period palazzo with a grand entrance and stairway. Dorm beds are available.

Hotel Ginevra
MAP R1 ▪ Via Genova 116 ▪ 081 28 32 10 ▪ www. hotelginevra.it ▪ €
Positioned just outside the station, this *pensione* is an oasis of calm.

Hotel Piazza Bellini
MAP N2 ▪ Via S Maria di Costantinopoli 101 ▪ 081 45 17 32 ▪ www.hotel piazzabellini.com ▪ €
The comfortable rooms feature stylish, private bathrooms and modern decor with wooden floors and colourful artwork on the walls. The hotel is handy for Piazza Bellini and for all the sights of the old centre. A buffet breakfast is included and free Wi-Fi is available in the public areas.

Hotel Plaza Napoli
Piazza Principe Umberto I 23 ▪ 081 563 61 68 ▪ www. hotelplazanapoli.it ▪ €
Away from the main hubbub, this Best Western hotel offers most of the features expected of this good-value American chain: hairdryers, safes, minibars, lifts, air conditioning and the like.

Hotel San Pietro
MAP Q3 ▪ Via San Pietro ad Aram ▪ 081 28 60 40 ▪ www.sanpietrohotel.it ▪ €
This hotel is located in historic Naples near museums, stations and shops. The rooms are well-furnished and clean, and staff are on call 24 hours a day. Free parking available at a nearby garage.

Capri Gems

Villa Eva
MAP S1 ▪ Via La Fabbrica 8, Anacapri ▪ 081 837 15 49 ▪ www.villaeva.com ▪ No air conditioning ▪ €
This paradise, close to the Blue Grotto, has an array of accommodation, and a pool *(see p61)*.

Villa Krupp
MAP T2 ▪ Viale Matteotti 12 ▪ 081 837 03 62 ▪ www.villakrupp.com ▪ €
Situated above the Gardens of Augustus, this white-washed stone villa used to be Maxim Gorky's house. A more panoramic position would be hard to find, even on this island. Beautifully decorated, in the light-suffused Capri way, with antiques appropriate to its historic importance.

Villa Sarah
MAP U1 ▪ Via Tiberio 3/A ▪ 081 837 78 17 ▪ www.villasarah.it ▪ €
Located up towards Villa Jovis *(see p34)* from the busy centre of Capri, this is a bucolic retreat. The hotel's hillside position affords spectacular views of the island and the sea. The old villa has been beautifully converted, with antique details left just as they were, such as the well in the patio.

Weber Ambassador

MAP T2 ■ Via Marina Piccola ■ 081 837 01 41 ■ www.hotelweber.com ■ €

With its commanding position overlooking this little port and beach, this hotel makes a perfect hideaway. The many terraces at several levels afford magnificent views of the famous I Faraglioni rocks, and the beach is just steps away from all this 4-star luxury.

Bellavista

MAP T1 ■ Via Orlandi 10, Anacapri ■ 081 837 14 63 ■ www.bellavistacapri. com ■ DA ■ €€

Vine-covered walkways surround the main hotel building, and the rooms are airy and well-appointed.

A Pazziella

MAP U1 ■ Via Fuorlovado 36 ■ 081 837 00 44 ■ www.royalgroup.it/ apazziella/it ■ €€

The overall impression here is light-filled freshness, cool colours and serenity, yet it's just a few steps away from the highlife in La Piazzetta and the shops and restaurants. A wonderful place for a Capri sojourn.

Capri Palace Hotel and Spa

MAP U1 ■ Via Capodimonte 2b ■ 081 978 01 11 ■ www.capri palace.com ■ DA ■ €€€

After a makeover the comfort at the Capri Palace is astounding. The beauty and spa treatments are excellent. There's a large swimming pool and some suites even have their own pools. The hotel's L'Olivo is a Michelin-starred restaurant.

Grand Hotel Quisisana

MAP U1 ■ Via Camerelle 2 ■ 081 837 07 88 ■ www. quisi.com ■ €€€

This is the jewel in the crown of Capri exclusivity, opulence, attention to detail and sheer scale. Restaurants, lounges, private rooms, pools and gardens, are all serenely beautiful. There's also a fitness centre.

Hotel Caesar Augustus

MAP T1 ■ Via G Orlandi 4, Anacapri ■ 081 837 33 95 ■ www.caesar-augustus. com ■ DA ■ €€€

The Caesar Augustus takes its place among the finest accommodation options in the world. Its terrace dazzles with its position above the bay.

JK Capri

MAP U1 ■ Via Marina Grande 225 ■ 081 838 41 11 ■ www.jkcapri.com ■ €€€

Standing proud above the port and painted white, this luxury hotel makes a conscious effort to recall the island's ancient heritage – this spot is where the Emperor Tiberius had one of his villas. There is private access to a small beach as well as a heated outdoor swimming pool. Breakfast is included.

Sorrentine Peninsula Sojourns

Hotel La Primavera, Massa Lubrense

MAP D5 ■ Via IV Novembre 3G ■ 081 878 91 25 ■ www.laprima vera.biz ■ €

This small restaurant-hotel, perched on a rocky spur, enjoys great views and is surrounded by lush olive groves.

Hotel Savoia, Sorrento

MAP D5 ■ Via Fuorimura 46 ■ 081 878 25 11 ■ www.savoia-hotel.com ■ €

Ideally located in the centre of Sorrento, this quaint family-run hotel is within walking distance of the beach and provides easy access to shops, restaurants and public transport. A delicious hot and cold breakfast buffet is included in the price.

Nice, Sorrento

MAP D5 ■ Corso Italia 257 ■ 081 878 16 50 ■ www.hotelnice sorrento.com ■ €

Small, simply furnished, and centrally located, this modest hotel is just a few blocks from the main square of Sorrento.

Piccolo Paradiso, Massa Lubrense

MAP D5 ■ Piazza Madonna della Lobra 5, Marina di Lobra ■ 081 878 92 40 ■ www.piccolo-paradiso.com ■ €

A simple yet well laid-out hotel with a lovely pool and stunning sea views.

La Tonnarella, Sorrento

MAP D5 ■ Via Capo 31 ■ 081 878 11 53 ■ www. latonnarella.it ■ €

With its clifftop setting and elegant interiors, this is an amazing find; it fills up very fast, so book in advance. Guests can enjoy the pleasant private beach and a good restaurant in a wonderful glass-walled setting with panoramas of the bay.

For a key to hotel price categories see p126

Bellevue Syrene, Sorrento

MAP D5 ▪ Piazza della Vittoria 5 ▪ 081 878 10 24 ▪ www.bellevue.it ▪ DA ▪ €€

Built on the ruins of a 2nd-century BC Roman villa, this pretty hotel carries the Roman theme forward with Pompeian decor in some rooms and even a Jacuzzi that has been made to resemble a Roman bath.

Grand Hotel La Medusa, Castellammare di Stabia

MAP E4 ▪ Via Passeggiata Archeologica 5 ▪ 081 872 33 83 ▪ www.lamedusa hotel.com ▪ DA ▪ €€

This grand country villa has an array of elegant touches, from terracotta vases adorning the gate to the busts of Roman emperors, as well as gardens, fountains and a pool. Rooms are spacious and the dining is superb.

Hotel Capo La Gala, Vico Equense

MAP D4 ▪ Via Luigi Serio 8, Scrajo ▪ 081 879 87 47 ▪ www.capolagala.com ▪ Open Apr–Oct ▪ €€

In a stunning spot along the Sorrentine Coast, this resort is hewn out of the living rock. There are only 22 rooms, each with a sea view and guests have access to sulphur baths, a private beach and a good restaurant.

Grand Hotel Excelsior Vittoria, Sorrento

MAP D5 ▪ Piazza Tasso 34 ▪ 081 877 71 11 ▪ www. exvitt.it ▪ DA ▪ €€€

Historic and utterly beautiful, with its clifftop position, extensive well-manicured gardens and grounds, and lavish public and private spaces. One of the world's best.

Imperial Hotel Tramontano, Sorrento

MAP D5 ▪ Via Veneto 1 ▪ 081 878 25 88 ▪ www. hoteltramontano.it ▪ DA ▪ €€€

This is another fabulous property, built on top of a Roman villa and frequented by the great and regal. Guests have included Romantic poets Shelley and Byron. A pool, gardens and striking panoramas render it as unforgettable today as it was in Grand Tour times.

Amalfi Coast Stays

Lidomare, Amalfi

MAP E4 ▪ Largo Piccolomini ▪ 089 87 13 32 ▪ www.lidomare.it ▪ No air conditioning ▪ €

A charming, family-run *pensione* with mostly large, airy rooms, tiled floors and antique furniture.

Luna Convento, Amalfi

MAP E5 ▪ Via Pantaleone Comite 33 ▪ 089 87 10 02 ▪ www.lunahotel.it ▪ €€

This former convent has a unique position at one end of Amalfi, clinging to a cliff, with a fortified tower on the promontory that is now used for special events. The rooms are tiny but charming, and the pool is a big draw.

Villa Maria, Ravello

MAP E4 ▪ Via Trinità 14 ▪ 089 85 72 55 ▪ www. villamaria.it ▪ €€

This atmospheric villa offers cooking courses and boasts one of the best restaurants in town. There are superb vistas from the foyer.

Hotel Caruso, Ravello

MAP E4 ▪ Piazza San Giovanni del Toro 2 ▪ 089 85 88 01 ▪ www. hotelcaruso.com ▪ €€€

Housed in an 11th-century palace, touches of its original splendour abound. The view of the coastline from the infinity pool is breathtaking.

Hotel Palumbo and Palumbo Residence, Ravello

MAP E4 ▪ Via S Giovanni del Toro 16 ▪ 089 85 72 44 ▪ www.hotel-palumbo.it ▪ €€€

The 12th-century Palazzo Confalone has been converted into one of the area's finest hotels. Its fine architecture reveals Arabic and Oriental influences, and many of its columns are ancient Greek and Roman. The service is impeccable, while the views and the restaurant are unsurpassed.

Monastero Santa Rosa, Conca dei Marini

MAP E5 ▪ Via Roma 2 ▪ 089 832 11 99 ▪ www. monasterosantarosa.com ▪ €€€

Dramatically situated at the edge of a cliff overlooking the coastline, this former convent has been exquisitely trans-formed into a luxurious retreat, complete with terraced garden, top-notch spa and dreamy infinity pool. The refined decor is perfectly in keeping with the historic atmosphere and secluded setting.

Palazzo Avino, Ravello

MAP E4 ▪ Via S Giovanni del Toro 28 ▪ 089 81 81 81 ▪ www.palazzoavino. com ▪ €€€

Opened in 1997 in a 13th-century palace, the decor is a ravishing blend of Moorish and European elements. Other highlights include incredible views, a fabulous restaurant and a beach club.

San Pietro, Positano

MAP E5 ▪ Via Laurito 2 ▪ 089 87 54 55 ▪ www. ilsanpietro.it ▪ €€€

This five-star hotel is just east of Positano proper in an isolated spot. No fewer than 20 terraces, hewn out of the rock, feature individual guest rooms with private balconies and Jacuzzis. A lift takes guests down to the foyer from the car park, and a second lift delivers you to the private beach. Children under 10 not permitted.

Santa Caterina, Amalfi

MAP E5 ▪ Strada Amalfitana 9 ▪ 089 87 10 12 ▪ www.hotelsanta caterina.it ▪ €€€

Amalfi's finest hotel is perched on a clifftop above the town. Its beautifully appointed rooms and "honeymoon" suites are airy and decorated with antique furniture. Gardens, a pool, a lift to the private beach and two restaurants add to the overall luxury.

Le Sirenuse, Positano

MAP E5 ▪ Via Cristoforo Colombo 30 ▪ 089 87 50 66 ▪ www.sirenuse.it ▪ €€€

A palatial establishment that attracts well-heeled guests. It's decorated in signature Amalfi Coast style, with vibrant majolica tiles and antiques. The pool is small, but there is a gym, and the hotel restaurant is renowned.

Villa Cimbrone, Ravello

MAP E4 ▪ Via Sta Chiara 26 ▪ 089 85 74 59 ▪ www. villacimbrone.com ▪ €€€

Inimitably captivating with its frescoed ceilings, price-less antiques and amazing views and gardens.

Island Charmers

Casa Gentile Hotel, Procida

MAP B4 ▪ Marina Corricella 88 ▪ 081 896 77 99 ▪ No air conditioning ▪ €

Glowing pink at one end of the port, this attractive hotel is reached on foot down worn stone stairs. The rooms are spacious, and there's also a private pier where guests can anchor their boats.

Hotel Crescenzo, Procida

MAP B4 ▪ Marina della Chiaollella 33 ▪ 081 896 72 55 ▪ www.hotel crescenzo.it ▪ €

This little hotel is known as much for its excellent fish restaurant as for its accommodation. Some of the rooms give direct access onto the harbour.

Hotel Terme Punta del Sole, Ischia

MAP A4 ▪ Piazza Maltese, Forio ▪ 081 98 91 56 ▪ www.casthotels.com ▪ €

Situated in the heart of a quiet, flower-filled part of the island, this attractive hotel is not far away from sandy beaches and the famous Poseidon gardens. A tennis court and parking facilities are located nearby.

Il Monastero, Ischia

MAP A4 ▪ Castello Aragonese, Ischia Ponte ▪ 081 99 24 35 ▪ www. castelloaragonese.it ▪ No air conditioning ▪ €

This hotel occupies part of the monastery of the Castello itself. Conse-quently the rooms are quite basic, but the views are prized.

Villa Angelica, Ischia

MAP A4 ▪ Via IV Novembre 28, Lacco Ameno ▪ 081 99 45 24 ▪ www.villaangelica.it ▪ €

A sunlit setting, hospitality and Mediterranean archi-tecture is what greets you upon arrival. It has a spa, and the sea is on your doorstep.

B&B Villa Marinella, Ischia

MAP A4 ▪ Via Castiglione 66, Casamicciola Terme ▪ 091 842 07 54 ▪ www. villamarinellaischia.it ▪ €€

This elegant B&B is ideally located between the main ports of the island, Ischia Porto and Casamicciola Terme, and is also close to the thermal parks. The rooms are large and individually decorated. Bicycles available for hire.

La Casa sul Mare, Procida

MAP B4 ▪ Salita Castello 13, Corricella ▪ 081 896 87 99 ▪ www.lacasa sulmare.it ▪ €€

Housed in a renovated building dating from 1700, this hotel is at the foot of the acropolis of Terra Murata. Most rooms enjoy views of the picturesque fishing village.

For a key to hotel price categories see p126

Miramare e Castello, Ischia

MAP A4 ▪ Via Pontano 5, Ischia Ponte ▪ 081 99 13 33 ▪ www.miramare castello.alysandyischia. com ▪ €€

The premium rooms here have balconies with bay vistas, but all accommodation is on the beach and in sight of the Castello Aragonese. Other pluses include elegant public areas and lots of facilities – a spa and beauty centre, a private beach, and three swimming pools, one with thermal water.

Albergo Regina Isabella and Royal Sporting, Ischia

MAP A4 ▪ Piazza S Restituta 1, Lacco Ameno ▪ 081 99 43 22 ▪ www. reginaisabella.it ▪ €€€

This hotel may have been at its best in the 1950s, but it still has a charming air of sophistication. In a good location overlooking the sea, facilities include a swimmming pool jutting out over the beach and spa services.

Il Moresco Grand Hotel, Ischia

MAP A4 ▪ Via E Gianturco 16, Ischia Porto ▪ 081 98 13 55 ▪ www.ilmoresco.it ▪ €€€

The Neo-Moorish architecture, the spa and the careful service have made this hotel the meeting point of an international clientele. Situated in the most beautiful corner of the island, the refined villa is set in a lush green park surrounding a thermal pool, and is just a few steps away from its own private beach.

Agriturismos, Villas and B&Bs

Agriturismo Il Casale, Bacoli

MAP B4 ▪ Contrada Coste di Baia, Via Selvatico 12 ▪ 081 523 51 93 ▪ www. ilcasaleagriturismo.com ▪ No air conditioning ▪ €

The farmhouse here is actually situated in a volcano that died out over 10,000 years ago. In this impressive scenery, you can appreciate the changing of the seasons.

Agriturismo La Ginestra, Vico Equense

MAP D4 ▪ Via Tessa 2, Santa Maria del Castello ▪ 081 802 32 11 ▪ www.laginestra.org ▪ No air conditioning ▪ €

The farm's organically grown produce tempts most guests to sign on for half-board. The farmhouse has airy rooms, many of which have good views down to the sea.

Agriturismo Marecoccola, Sorrento

MAP D5 ▪ Via Malacoccola 10 ▪ 081 533 01 51 ▪ €

Amid citrus trees and countless paths to hidden beaches, this farm has been run by the same family for over a century. Minimum 3-night stay.

Casa Cosenza, Positano

MAP E5 ▪ Via Trara Genoino 18 ▪ 089 87 50 63 ▪ www.casacosenza.it ▪ €

A sunny B&B run by a local family, Casa Cosenza stands halfway down the Positano hillside, offering stunning views from its tiled terrace. The rooms vary – some have a balcony

or private terrace; all have en-suite bathrooms. Apartments are also available.

Il Giardino di Vigliano, Massa Lubrense

MAP D5 ▪ Località Villazzano ▪ 081 533 98 23 ▪ www.vigliano.org ▪ €

The name originates from Roman times, as does the site, and the panorama inspires poets even to this day. Lemon groves abound, their fragrance adding a sweet note to the air of total relaxation on offer at this villa.

Hotel Punta Chiarito, Ischia

MAP A4 ▪ Via Sorgeto 51, Forio ▪ 081 90 81 02 ▪ Closed Nov–Dec ▪ www.puntachiarito.it ▪ €

Given its spectacular position, it's little wonder that guests refer to the place as a paradise. It is surrounded by colourful and fragrant vegetation while a natural source of thermal water fills basins created with local stone.

Residence La Neffola, Sorrento

MAP D5 ▪ Via Capo 21 ▪ 081 878 13 44 ▪ www. neffolaresidence.com ▪ No air conditioning ▪ €

"Neffola" is the name of a fresh spring coming out of the rocks outside the town of Sorrento. This charming building has been restored and is surrounded by lovely gardens.

Il Roseto Resort, Sorrento

MAP D5 ▪ Corso Italia 304 ▪ 081 878 10 38 ▪ www. ilrosetosorrento.com ▪ €

Complete with a lush lemon-tree grove and a pool, this family-run B&B

offers a comfortable stay not far from the centre of Sorrento. The rooms have views overlooking the sea or the garden.

Il Vitigno, Ischia
MAP A4 ■ Via Bocca 31, Forio ■ 081 99 83 07 ■ www.ilvitigno.com ■ No air conditioning ■ €
This wonderfully earthy farm has a rustic rock-pool, a large terracotta tile terrace, and white-washed elegance. It is also known in the area for its excellent cuisine.

Hostels and Camping

Averno Camping, Pozzuoli
MAP C3 ■ Via Montenuovo Licola Patria 85, Arco Felice Lucrino ■ 081 804 26 66 ■ No air conditioning ■ €
Among the facilities on offer here are a tennis court, a pool, a Jacuzzi, a sauna, a bar, a restaurant, a gym and a disco. There are also bungalows to rent.

Camping Mirage, Ischia
MAP A4 ■ Via Marconi 37, Barano ■ 081 990 551 ■ www.campingmirage.it ■ No air conditioning ■ €
A great choice along the sandy beach known as Spiaggia dei Maronti.

Fabric Hostel, Naples
MAP L2 ■ Via Bellucci Sessa 22 ■ 081 776 58 74 ■ www.fabrichostel.com ■ €
Housed in a former fabric factory, this hostel is lively year-round, and with multi-lingual staff. It offers a variety of rooms that are available for families, singles or groups.

Hostel A' Scalinatella, Atrani
MAP E5 ■ Piazza Umberto I 5–6 ■ 089 87 14 92 ■ www.hostelscalinatella. com ■ No air conditioning ■ €
In this family-run operation there are dormitory rooms with private bathrooms, and apartments scattered all over town, up and down the staircases that serve as streets here.

Hostel Brikette, Positano
MAP E5 ■ Via G Marconi 358 ■ 089 87 58 57 ■ www.brikette.com ■ €
Decorated with mosaic tiles and the owner's murals, this eclectic hostel offers friendly and helpful service. A variety of rooms are available, including those with en-suite bath-rooms and sea views. Near a bus stop and only minutes from the beach.

Hostel delle Sirene, Sorrento
MAP D5 ■ Via degli Aranci 160 ■ 081 807 29 25 ■ www.hostellesirene. net ■ No credit cards ■ No air conditioning ■ €
This self-proclaimed "VIP backpacker" establish-ment is the best deal in town. Although short on views, it's convenient enough to everything of importance, and is right behind the train station.

Nube d'Argento Camping, Sorrento
MAP D5 ■ Via Capo 21 ■ 081 878 13 44 ■ www. nubedargento.com ■ No credit cards ■ No air conditioning ■ €
A pleasant camp site that enjoys views of Vesuvius. Facilities include pools and a restaurant.

Ostello Mergellina, Naples
Salita della Grotta a Piedigrotta 23 ■ 081 761 23 46 ■ DA ■ No credit cards ■ No air conditioning ■ €
This hostel may not be very central, but the district and the position are attractive in their own right. The rooms are well maintained and the staff is extremely friendly and helpful. Private double rooms are available and the evening meal is a real bargain for the area. Doors close early but a receptionist will let you in after curfew.

Vulcano Solfatara Camping, Pozzuoli
MAP C3 ■ Via Solfatara 161 ■ 081 526 74 13 ■ www.solfatara.it ■ No air conditioning ■ €
Services here include a bar, a swimming pool, and even a restaurant. For exploring the city of Naples, this is definitely the best camp site in the area, located conveniently near both a metro stop and the port of Pozzuoli for island trips in the area, as well. There are also independent bungalows for rent.

Zeus Camping, Pompeii
MAP E4 ■ Via Villa dei Misteri ■ 081 861 53 20 ■ www.campingzeus.it ■ DA ■ No credit cards ■ No air conditioning ■ €
Just steps away from the archaeological site, within the grounds of this verdant camp site you'll find a bar, a restaurant and shops. For those who prefer not to be under canvas, there are also bungalows for rent.

General Index

Acknowledgments

Author
American-born Jeffrey Kennedy now lives mainly in Italy and Spain. A graduate of Stanford University, he divides his time between producing, acting and writing. He is the co-author of Top 10 Rome and the author of the Top 10 guides to Mallorca, Miami and the Keys, San Francisco and Andalucia.

Additional Contributor
Laura Thayer

Publishing Director Georgina Dee

Publisher Vivien Antwi

Design Director Phil Ormerod

Editorial Michelle Crane, Rachel Fox, Ruth Reisenberger, Sally Schafer, Sophie Wright

Design Tessa Bindloss, Richard Czapnik

Commissioned Photography Demetrio Carrasco, Rough Guides/Karen Trist, Clive Streeter

Picture Research Susie Peachey, Ellen Root, Lucy Sienkowska, Oran Tarjan

Cartography Subhashree Bharti, Tom Coulson, Fabio Ratti Editoria, Suresh Kumar, James MacDonald

DTP Jason Little

Production Olivia Jeffries

Factchecker Alessandra Pugliese

Proofreader Leena Lane

Indexer Helen Peters

First edition created by Blue Island Publishing, London

Revisions Team
Parnika Bagla, Alice Fewery, Vinita Venugopal

Picture Credits
The publisher would like to thank the following for their kind permission to reproduce their photographs:
Key: a-above; b-below/bottom; c-centre; f-far; l-left; r-right; t-top

123RF.com: Jennifer Barrow 87tl; perseomedusa 113cl.

4Corners: SIME//Massimo Borchi 53cl, /Pietro Canali 61cr, 65b, /Antonio Capone 55cl, /Demma 72tl, /Giovanni Simeone 58tl.

Alamy Stock Photo: age fotostock/Christian Goupi 50tl, /Pietro Scozzari 72bl; AGF Srl Antonio Capone 52cl, 69clb, 73bl; Jennifer Barrow 4crb; Giuseppe Bartuccio 71tr; Mark Bassett 4cr; Blend Images/ac productions 69br; blickwinkel 2tr, 40-1; Bon Appetit/Alexandra Grablewski 93crb; Massimiliano Bonatti 85bl; Massimo Buonaiuto 78br; Julia Catt Photography 28tl; Robin Chapman 67br; Alfredo Consentino 115crb; Richard Cummins 14br; Collection Dagli Orti 47cra; Design Pics Inc /Richard Cummins 15cr; Adam Eastland 27tl, 83cra; Elenaphotos 54t, 106cla; FC_Italy 29tr; funkyfood London/Paul Williams 11crb; GL Archive 20tr; Granger, NYC. 42tc; hemis.fr/ Camille Moirenc 98-9, / Ludovic Maisant 13tr, 13cr, /René Mattes 59tl, 108tr; Heritage Image Partnership Ltd/Fine Art Images *Maria Amalia of Saxony], Queen of Naples* by Bonito, Giuseppe 96cra; John Heseltine 30cl; imageBROKER/Bahnmueller 114bl, /Erich Schmidt 59br; Massimo Lama 64cl; Lebrecht Music and Arts Photo Library/*The Sicilian Vespers* by Barabino 42b; LOOK Die Bildagentur der Fotografen GmbH /Hauke Dressler 4cl; MARKA/ Massimiliano Bonatti 93cla; Barry Mason 4b; Mayday 58b; nagelestock.com 1; PAINTING/ National Museum of Capodimonte, Naples/*Judith Slaying Holofernes* by Artemisia Gentileschi 22br; Pacific Press/Emanuele Sessa 73tr; REDA &CO srl/Alfio Giannotti 38bc; Francesca Sciarra 6br; Eugene Sergeev 100c; Neil Setchfield 63cr; Sites & Photos/Capture Ltd 18crb; Stock Italia 33clb; The Art Archive/ Collection Dagli Orti 4clb; Ivan Vdovin 11tl, 22r, 29cl, 39tl, 48t, 96bl; Visions of America, LLC/ Joseph Sohm 56-7; Christine Webb 81cra, 83bl; World History Archive 45tr; Ernst Wrba 68bl, 71cl.

AWL Images: Demetrio Carrasco 58cr.

Bowinkel: Uberto Bowinkel 91tl.

Bridgeman Images: Look and Learn 43cl.

Corbis: Atlantide Phototravel/Massimo Borchi 34cl; Bettmann 33crb; Design Pics/Jon Spaull 84cra; Leemage 18-9, 78cla; Tuul & Bruno Morandi 46tl; Ocean/68/Buena Vista Images 66cl; SOPA/Kaos02 60b, 111tl.

Da Paolino Lemon Trees: 109bl.

Dreamstime.com: Adreslebedev 11br; Agneskantaruk 67cl; Alexchered 62cl; Amoklv 36-7; Baloncici 52b; Jennifer Barrow 30-1, 60tl; Beriliu 10cra; Vincenzo De Bernardo 61tl; Blitzkoenig 35cb; Ciolca 49br, 105clb; Wessel Cirkel 33tl, 94cla, 95br; Conde 51cl; Dennis Dolkens 12-3; Elen 50b; Faberfoto 36clb; Fedecandoniphoto 69tl; Sergii Figurnyi 102cla; Freesurf69 4t, 104tl; Frenta 2tl, 8-9; Janos Gaspar 24-5, 37cr, 102br; Gigavisual 38-9; Francesco Riccardo Iacomino 3tl, 74-5; Vladimir Korostyshevskiy 20bl, 26cla, 26br, 73cl, 86cla, 87br; Lachris77 10cl, 14cl, 88b; Leonardoboss 101tr; Lukaszimilena 7tl; Rosario Manzo 3tr, 10br, 88tl, 116-7; Merlin1812 32br; Milosk50 112tr, 114cl; minnystock 4cla, 27-6, 55tr, 103cl; MNStudio 68c, 81cb; Danilo Mongiello 112cl; Anna Pakutina 76tl; Photogolfer 10c, 77tl, 80t, 89cl; Enrico Della Pietra 14-5, 16cl; Angela Ravaioli 112bl; Michele Renzullo 31cb; Sarra22 12bl, 23cb; Scaliger 11cra, 54bl, 70br; Oleksii Skopiuk 16-7b, 17cb; Slasta20 66tr; Smilemf 7clb; Andrei Stancu 34crb; Danilo Szywangruber 11c, 34-5; Ttatty 111br; Vacclav 95t.

Getty Images: De Agostini Picture Library 18cla, 22cl, 33tr, /Archivio J. Lange 10clb, /A. Dagli

Orti19br; Lonely Planet 82tr, 92bl; Mondadori Portfolio 28b; Sergio Anelli/Electa /Mondadori Portfolio 23tl; UIG/Leemage 21clb; Peter Unger 30crb; Eric Vandeville 32cl.

Milleunaceramica: 106bc.

Museo Archeologico di Pithecusae: 49c.

Museo MADRE, Naples: *Axér / Desaxér* (2015) by Daniel Buren, photo Amedeo Benestante 63tl.

Museo Nazionale Ferroviario di Pietrarsa: Giuseppe Senese 64tr.

Museobottega della Tarsialignea: 48bc.

Ospedale delle Bambole: Roberto Jandoli 65cr.

Il Principe: 97cr.

Rex by Shutterstock: Courtesy Everett Collection 46cr, 46bl; imageBROKER 12cr, 62br; Miramax/Everett 47cla; Paramount/Everett 47bl; UIG/ Photoservice Electa 44br.

Robert Harding Picture Library: Arco Images GmbH/R. Kiedrowski 34bc; Peter Barritt 21tr; Helmut Corneli 70t; Alfio Giannotti 110cla; Olivier Goujon 37tc; R. Kiedrowski 107tr; Ivan Vdovin 51tr; Ernst Wrba 14crb.

Photo Scala, Florence: courtesy of Curia Vescovile di Napoli 16-7; DeAgostini Picture Library 17tl, /Sammlungen des Fuersten von Liechtenstein, Vaduz, Liechtenstein/ *Portrait of the Royal Family of Naples. Ferdinand IV of the Two Sicilies (Naples, 1751-1825) and his Wife Maria Carolina of Austria (1752-1814) with their Sons* (1783) by Angelica Kauffmann 43br; Fondo Edifici di Culto - Min. dell'Interno 44tl; courtesy of the Ministero Beni e Att. Culturali 19tc, 28c, / Museo di San Martino, Naples/*Gratitude for ceasing the plague* by Gargiulo, Domenico (called Micco Spadaro 1612-1679) 43tl, Certosa di San Martino, Naples/ *Triumph of Judith* by Luca Giordano 44cl.

Teatro Bellini: 90crb.

Cover
Front and spine: **Getty Images:** Francesco Iacobelli.

Back: **Dreamstime.com:** V0v.

Pull Out Map Cover
Getty Images: Francesco Iacobelli

All other images © Dorling Kindersley
For further information see:
www.dkimages.com

Penguin Random House

Printed and bound in China

First American Edition, 2004
Published in the United States by
DK Publishing, 345 Hudson Street,
New York, New York 10014

Copyright 2004, 2016 © Dorling Kindersley Limited

A Penguin Random House Company

16 17 18 19 20 10 9 8 7 6 5 4 3 2 1

Reprinted with revisions 2006, 2008, 2010, 2012, 2014, 2016

Published in Great Britain by Dorling Kindersley Limited.

A catalog record for this book is available from the Library of Congress.

ISSN 1479-344X

ISBN 978 1 4654 5744 8

MIX
Paper from responsible sources
FSC™ C018179

SPECIAL EDITIONS OF DK TRAVEL GUIDES

DK Travel Guides can be purchased in bulk quantities at discounted prices for use in promotions or as premiums. We are also able to offer special editions and personalized jackets, corporate imprints, and excerpts from all of our books, tailored specifically to meet your own needs.

To find out more, please contact:

in the US
specialsales@dk.com

in the UK
travelguides@uk.dk.com

in Canada
specialmarkets@dk.com

in Australia
**penguincorporatesales@
penguinrandomhouse.com.au**

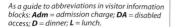
*As a guide to abbreviations in visitor information blocks: **Adm** = admission charge; **DA** = disabled access; **D** = dinner; **L** = lunch.*

Phrase Book

In an Emergency

Help!	Aiuto!	eye-yoo-toh
Stop!	Ferma!	fair-mah
Call a doctor	Chiama un medico	kee-ah-mah oon meh-deekoh
Call an ambulance	Chiama un' ambulanza	kee-ah-mah oon am-boo-lan-tsa
Call the police	Chiama la polizia	kee-ah-mah lah pol-ee-tsee-ah
Call the fire brigade	Chiama i pompieri	kee-ah-mah ee pom-pee-air-ee

Communication Essentials

Yes/No	Sì/No	see/noh
Please	Per favore	pair fah-vor-eh
Thank you	Grazie	grah-tsee-eh
Excuse me	Mi scusi	mee skoo-zee
Hello	Buongiorno	bwon jor-noh
Goodbye	Arrivederci	ah-ree-veh-dair-chee
Good evening	Buona sera	bwon-ah sair-ah
What?	Che?	keh
When?	Quando?	kwan-doh
Why?	Perchè?	pair-keh
Where?	Dove?	doh-veh

Useful Phrases

How are you?	Come sta?	koh-meh stah
Very well, thank you.	Molto bene, grazie.	moll-toh beh-neh grah-tsee-eh
Pleased to meet you.	Piacere di conoscerla.	pee-ah-chair-eh dee coh-noh-shair-lah
That's fine.	Va bene.	va beh-neh
Where is/ are…?	Dov'è/ Dove sono…?	dov-eh/ doveh soh-noh
How do I get to…?	Come faccio per arrivare a…?	koh-meh fah-cho pair arri-var-eh a
Do you speak English?	Parla inglese?	par-lah een-gleh-zeh
I don't understand.	Non capisco.	non ka-pee-skoh
I'm sorry.	Mi dispiace.	mee dee-spee-ah-cheh

Shopping

How much does this cost?	Quant'è, per favore?	kwan-teh pair fah-vor-eh
I would like…	Vorrei…	vor-ray
Do you have…?	Avete…?	ah-veh-teh
Do you take credit cards?	Accettate carte di credito?	ah-chet-tah-teh kar-teh dee creh-dee-toh
What time do you open/close?	A che ora apre/ chiude?	a keh ora ah-preh/ kee-oo-deh
this one	questo	kweh-stoh
that one	quello	kwell-oh
expensive	caro	kar-oh
cheap	economico	ee-con-om-ee-coh
size (clothes)	la taglia	lah tah-lee-ah
size (shoes)	il numero	eel noo-mair-oh
white	bianco	bee-ang-koh
black	nero	neh-roh
red	rosso	ross-oh
yellow	giallo	jal-loh
green	verde	vair-deh
blue	blu	bloo

Types of Shop

bakery	il forno/ panificio	eel forn-oh/ panee-fee-cho
bank	la banca	lah bang-kah
bookshop	la libreria	lah lee-breh-ree-ah
cake shop	la pasticceria	lah pas-tee-chair-ee-ah
chemist	la farmacia	lah far-mah-chee-ah
delicatessen	la salumeria	lah sah-loo-meh-ree-ah
department store	il grande magazzino	eel gran-deh ma-gad-zeenoh
grocery	alimentari	ah-lee-men-tah-ree
hairdresser	il parrucchiere	eel par-oo-kee-air-eh
ice-cream parlour	la gelateria	lah jel-lah-tair-ree-ah
market	il mercato	eel mair-kah-toh
newsstand	l'edicola	leh-dee-koh-lah
post office	l'ufficio postale	loo-fee-choh pos-tah-leh
supermarket	il supermercato	eel su-pair-mair-kah-toh
tobacconist	il tabaccaio	eel tah-bak-eye-oh
travel agency	l'agenzia di viaggi	lah-jen-tsee-ah dee vee-ad-jee

Sightseeing

art gallery	la pinacoteca	lah peena-koh-teh-kah
bus stop	la fermata dell'autobus	lah fair-mah-tah dell-ow-toh-booss
church	la chiesa/ basilica	lah kee-eh-zah bah-seel-ee-kah
closed for holidays	chiuso per ferie	kee-oo-zoh pair fair-ee-eh
garden	il giardino	eel jar-dee-no
museum	il museo	eel moo-zeh-oh
railway station	la stazione	lah stah-tsee-oh-neh
tourist information	l'ufficio del turismo	loo-fee-choh del too-ree-smoh

Staying in a Hotel

Do you have any vacant rooms?	Avete camere libere?	ah-veh-teh kah-mair-eh lee-bair-eh
double room	una camera doppia	oona kah-mairah doh-pee-ah
with double bed	con letto matrimoniale	kon let-toh mah-tree-moh-nee-ah-leh
a room with bath/ shower	una camera con bagno/ doccia	oona ka-mair-ah kon ban-yoh/ dot-chah
twin room	una camera con due letti	oona kah-mairah kon doo-eh let-tee

single room	una camera singola	oona kah-mairah sing-goh-lah
I have a reservation	Ho fatto una prenotazione	oh fat-toh oona preh-noh-tah-tsee-oh-neh

Eating Out

Have you got a table for…?	Avete un tavolo per…?	ah-veh-teh oon tah-voh-loh pair
I'd like to reserve a table	Vorrei prenotare un tavolo	vor-ray pre-noh-ta-reh oon tah-voh-loh
breakfast	colazione	koh-lah-tsee-oh-neh
lunch	pranzo	pran-tsoh
dinner	cena	cheh-nah
the bill	il conto	eel kon-toh
waitress	cameriera	kah-mair-ee-air-ah
waiter	cameriere	kah-mair-ee-air-eh
fixed-price menu	il menù a prezzo fisso	eel meh-noo ah pret-soh fee-soh
dish of the day	piatto del giorno	pee-ah-toh dell jor-no
starter	l'antipasto	lan-tee-pass-toh
first course	il primo	eel pree-moh
main course	il secondo	eel seh-kon-doh
vegetables	i contorni	ee kon-tor-noh
dessert	il dolce	eel doll-cheh
wine list	la lista dei vini	lah lee-stah day vee-nee
glass	il bicchiere	eel bee-kee-air-eh
bottle	la bottiglia	lah bot-teel-yah
knife	il coltello	eel kol-tell-oh
fork	la forchetta	lah for-ket-tah
spoon	il cucchiaio	eel koo-kee-eye-oh

Menu Decoder

l'acqua minerale	lah-kwah meenair-ah-leh	mineral water
gassata/ naturale	gah-zah-tah/ nah-too-rah-leh	fizzy/ still
agnello	ah-niell-oh	lamb
aglio	al-ee-oh	garlic
al forno	al for-noh	baked
alla griglia	ah-lah greel-yah	grilled
la birra	lah beer-rah	beer
la bistecca	lah bee-stek-ah	steak
il burro	eel boor-oh	butter
il caffè	eel kah-feh	coffee
la carne	la kar-neh	meat
carne di maiale	kar-neh dee mah-yah-leh	pork
la cipolla	la chip-oh-lah	onion
il formaggio	eel for-mad-joh	cheese
le fragole	leh frah-goh-leh	strawberries
il fritto misto	eel free-toh mees-toh	mixed fried seafood
la frutta	la froot-tah	fruit
frutti di mare	froo-tee dee mah-reh	seafood
i funghi	ee foon-ghee	mushrooms
i gamberi	ee gam-bair-ee	prawns
il gelato	eel jel-lah-toh	ice cream

l'insalata	leen-sah-lah-tah	salad
il latte	eel laht-teh	milk
il manzo	eel man-tsoh	beef
l'olio	loh-lee-oh	oil
il pane	eel pah-neh	bread
le patate	leh pah-tah-teh	potatoes
le patatine fritte	leh pah-tah-teen-eh free-teh	chips
il pepe	eel peh-peh	pepper
il pesce	eel pesh-eh	fish
il pollo	eel poll-oh	chicken
il pomodoro	eel poh-moh-dor-oh	tomato
il prosciutto cotto/ crudo	eel pro-shoo-toh kot-toh/ kroo-doh	ham cooked/ cured
il riso	eel ree-zoh	rice
il sale	eel sah-leh	salt
la salsiccia	lah sal-see-chah	sausage
il succo d'arancia	eel soo-koh dah-ran-chah	orange juice
il tè	eel teh	tea
la torta	lah tor-tah	cake/tart
l'uovo	loo-oh-voh	egg
vino bianco	vee-noh bee-ang-koh	white wine
vino rosso	vee-noh ross-oh	red wine
lo zucchero	loh zoo-kair-oh	sugar
la zuppa	lah tsoo-pah	soup

Time

one minute	un minuto	oon mee-noo-toh
one hour	un'ora	oon or ah
a day	un giorno	oon jor-noh
Monday	lunedì	loo-neh-dee
Tuesday	martedì	mar-teh-dee
Wednesday	mercoledì	mair-koh-leh-dee
Thursday	giovedì	joh-veh-dee
Friday	venerdì	ven-air-dee
Saturday	sabato	sah-bah-toh
Sunday	domenica	doh-meh-nee-ka

Numbers

1	uno	oo-noh
2	due	doo-eh
3	tre	treh
4	quattro	kwat-roh
5	cinque	ching-kweh
6	sei	say-ee
7	sette	set-teh
8	otto	ot-toh
9	nove	noh-veh
10	dieci	dee-eh-chee
11	undici	oon-dee-chee
17	diciassette	dee-chah-set-teh
18	diciotto	dee-chot-toh
19	diciannove	dee-chu-noh-veh
20	venti	ven-tee
30	trenta	tren-tah
40	quaranta	kwah-ran-tah
50	cinquanta	ching-kwan-tah
60	sessanta	sess-an-tah
70	settanta	set-tan-tah
80	ottanta	ot-tan-tah
90	novanta	noh-van-tah
100	cento	chen-toh
1,000	mille	mee-leh

144 » Street Index

Selected Naples Street Index